The Scribe Eadwine, a miniature from the Eadwine Psalter,
a 12th century English manuscript

A Short History of English Literature

by

Gilbert Phelps

The Folio Society

London 1962

PRINTED IN GREAT BRITAIN
Printed and bound by Jarrold & Sons Ltd, Norwich
Set in 'Monotype' Baskerville 11 point leaded 1½ points

Contents

Illustrations

Preface

THIS book sets out to tell the story of English literature from *Beowulf* to the 1930s by means of the broad general themes, as they present themselves to one individual observer. Inevitably this has its dangers. The best approach to literature is from the concrete to the abstract; from the study, that is, of specific works to conclusions based upon them. Those reached in any other way are bound to appear personal, arbitrary, or downright wrong-headed. In addition the facts that *are* chosen as pegs upon which to hang the generalizations, will assume a prominence at times out of proportion to their intrinsic value, and the resulting picture may look hopelessly lop-sided. Nevertheless it is an approach that at least avoids the catalogue effect of the 'potted history'. It is for this reason indeed that dates, names and titles have been kept to a minimum and that index, notes and book-lists have been omitted —for it is a book that is primarily meant to be read and enjoyed by the general reader as a consecutive story, rather than to be studied as a handbook to examinations in 'Eng. Lit.'.

At the same time it is hoped that as an introduction to English literature it will prove of value to the student too, and although it is very much a 'personal perspective' it does try to avoid at least some of the temptations of the subjective approach—and it is for that reason that the survey ends on the eve of the second world war with writers who may already be considered as belonging to literary history.

The attempt to summarize a nation's literature, unsatisfactory though it is in so many ways, may sometimes produce unexpected clarifications and insights: the imposition of an appearance of pattern and coherence (even if in fact it is no more than an appearance) can, moreover, act as a challenge and stimulus—and this book will certainly have achieved its purpose if in sketching outlines and contours it draws the explorer into the country and gives him heart to travel deeper—even if in the long run he discards every one of the original readings and ends up with an entirely different map of his own making.

A
Short History
of
English Literature

1 · Before and after Chaucer

ENGLISH literature is usually thought of as beginning with Geoffrey Chaucer. In many important respects this is true. It was not until his advent that an English literature came into being in which the modern reader can participate. It is possible for him to enjoy a page of Chaucer without too much difficulty: with a passage from our earlier literature he is virtually in the presence of a foreign language.

In fact there were more than six hundred years of written literature in these islands before Chaucer was born (not to mention the vast body of oral literature that had existed for hundreds, perhaps thousands, of years before that). This is a span roughly equal to that from Chaucer's death to the present day. To ignore those earlier centuries may be understandable in view of their strangeness, but it hardly makes for a balanced view.

If they are taken into account, however, the starting-point in the history of English literature must be *Beowulf*. It is true that the story of this epic (and it deserves this title) was brought to this country by the invading Angles in the sixth century—and has nothing to do with it: indeed it is not even about the Angles themselves, but about the Scandinavians. But it was in England that the story was made into a poem—about the year A.D. 700—and by the time it was set down in a manuscript some three hundred years later it had taken on a very characteristic stamp and had only an indirect relation to the pagan original.

For the Anglo-Saxon poems that have come down to us, *Beowulf* among them (they are preserved in four manuscripts attributed to the eleventh century), were written down by clerks after the conversion of the Anglo-Saxons to Christianity. If these clerks did not actually create Anglo-Saxon literature, they preserved it—and in doing so Christianized it. This, of course, was part of the Church's general policy of trying to absorb the pagan religions and their attendant myths and legends and to effect a synthesis of old and new. Thus even *Beowulf*, the only extant poem which conveys a picture of the primitive age on a large scale, has marked didactic elements and its hero at times appears almost as a Christian knight of the age of chivalry.

But though the clerks introduced Christian elements into the old stories, they also tended to look back to the exploits of their Viking forefathers with a feeling of nostalgia. Their adaptations of the pagan originals, therefore, were Christian and didactic in approach, but elegiac in tone.

This melancholy preoccupation with a dream of the past is one of the recurrent characteristics of our literature. Sometimes it was to become attached to Celtic sentiment, and in this connexion it is interesting to remember that some of the greatest centres of learning and culture in Anglo-Saxon times were the monasteries of Celtic monks. The same feeling occurs in some of the writers of the Romantic Revival in the first half of the nineteenth century, and in those of 'the Celtic twilight' in the latter half.

In view of the fact that the work of transcription was carried out by clerks in Holy orders it is not surprising that most of the poems they chose to preserve were of a religious nature—paraphrases of Biblical stories, lives of the saints, and so on. Indeed it cannot be too strongly stressed that the origins of our written literature were predominantly Christian, and that Christian modes of thought and feeling were to permeate it for centuries to come. When we remember that during the whole of this early period these islands were prey to successive invasions, so that spells of enlightenment alternated with spells of almost total barbarism, it must have seemed that Christianity—quite apart from its purely religious aspects—was the one bright hope for a civilized way of life. It was small wonder therefore that the clergy preached its doctrines and precepts so passionately or that so much of our early literature was didactic in purpose. It is here indeed that we have the origins of one of its most persistent—and sometimes one of its most irritating—characteristics.

These early religious poems, though they include some very interesting examples of the blending of Viking seascapes and battle-scenes with Christian mythology, are on the whole artistically inferior to the poems that were truly pagan in origin. But some of them (and particularly a poem about Judith and Holofernes) reveal considerable powers of characterization and of dramatic narration, and there is another about the fall of the rebel angels into Hell which may have been one of the inspirational sources of Milton's *Paradise Lost*.

There are two characteristics which all of the Anglo-Saxon poems have in common, both of them deriving from the nature of the language itself. The first of these is the long line in which they

An illustration from an 11th century manuscript of the Anglo-Saxon
poem of *Caedmon*

Bede's *Historia Ecclesiastica Anglorum*; a page from a late 8th century manuscript

were written, a line which depends not upon rhyme but upon alliteration—a metrical device natural to a language in which consonants were predominant. The second, deriving this time from the fact that Anglo-Saxon was poor in suffixes and prefixes, is the fondness for composite-words. The first of these made for a good deal of monotony. The second led to another fault: for while some of the composite words—such as 'bone chamber' for the body and 'the whale's road' for the sea (these are of course translated from the Anglo-Saxon forms)—are in themselves poetically vivid, their frequent use produces an effect of over-ornamentation.

The habit of periphrasis (for the process which originated in the exigencies of the language came to affect a whole way of thinking) even influenced the style of those clerics who wrote in Latin, though the greatest of them, the Venerable Bede, used a simple and vigorous Latin for his great *Historia Ecclesiastica Anglorum*, besides writing, and encouraging others to write, verses in the vernacular.

But although these two characteristics strike us as the most archaic of all—and the most remote from the varied and fluent versification of Geoffrey Chaucer—they were not altogether lost to our literature. Thus Gerard Manley Hopkins towards the end of the nineteenth century used 'picture words' as well as some metrical devices not dissimilar from those of the Anglo-Saxon poets.

It must be admitted, too, that the proneness to over-elaboration evident in these Anglo-Saxon writings was never to be entirely eliminated, so that in several periods of our literature there have to all intents and purposes been two distinct styles—the natural or idiomatic—and the self-consciously 'literary'.

The prose of this early period would present the modern reader with nothing like the same difficulty as the poetry. The main reason is that whereas the poetry was deliberately archaic, the prose was closer to everyday speech and everyday needs, though some of it was strongly influenced by the constructions of Latin. The great name in prose is that of King Alfred, who after his final defeat of the Danes in A.D. 896 or 897 set out to re-educate his people and, to that end, translated or caused to be translated a number of Latin works, including Bede's *Historia Ecclesiastica Anglorum*. It was Alfred, too, who probably started the historical annals known as the *Anglo-Saxon Chronicle*. Although his work and that of the patriots and educationalists who succeeded him was eventually swallowed up in the darkness of the later Danish invasions, these pioneers had established prose as a medium worthy to take its place beside poetry. It is also worth noting that the prose of this early period included some examples, derived from classical and foreign sources, of what can fairly be described as fiction.

In spite, therefore, of all the barriers between ourselves and our Anglo-Saxon ancestors, their literature must be seen as part of our cultural heritage. It represents the prologue to the story of English literature; true, it is written in a foreign language, but it belongs to the same book.

The story proper begins with the Norman Conquest of 1066. At first it might have seemed as if the old Anglo-Saxon culture was going to disappear for good. French became the official tongue, while the language of the conquered people—which had begun to coalesce round the West Saxon dialect—fell apart into its various regional components. For a hundred years or so there was apparently very little writing of note in the vernacular, apart from a few pious works (which include some verse translations of the Psalms and of parts of the Bible) and some particularly vivid entries in the *Anglo-Saxon Chronicle*, which, oddly enough, continued until 1154. As a consequence the Anglo-Saxon monks turned increasingly to Latin, not only for religious and historical writings but also for poetry.

It is significant, however, that they tended to turn back to the inspiration of Bede rather than to the continental Latinists, while the spirit of their works (especially in the case of the historical chronicles) was strongly national. And of course there was one great difference between this conquest and those that had preceded it: whereas the earlier invaders had been barbarians, the Normans brought with them a fully formed and highly sophisticated culture from which the vanquished could not fail to benefit. For the first time the English tradition entered the mainstream of European culture, while the language itself, as a result of numerous borrowings from the French, gradually became more supple and fluent. At the same time, the conquerors (who after all were also descendants of the Norsemen) were gradually absorbed into their new environment and it was not long before Anglo-Norman writings—though still composed in French—began to show tendencies very different from those of continental France. Many of them, for example, were almost as didactic in tone and approach as the old Anglo-Saxon literature. What is more, many of the Anglo-Norman metrical chronicles, though the vogue came from France, set out to explore the ancient legends of the different regions and races of Britain and to effect a fusion between them—and in the process found themselves expressing a new Anglo-Norman patriotism.

The body of legends that most interested them was that dealing with the legendary British King Arthur. The link here is through the ancient Celtic civilization which had spread over a large part of Western Europe. Many of the tales about Arthur originated in the Celtic parts of Britain, those least affected by the Saxon and Danish invasions, notably Cornwall and Wales: many more came from Brittany. There was a continuous interchange between the various Celtic areas and the tales were well known throughout France and in other parts of the Continent.

This burst of new interest in the Arthurian legends was important because they were to exercise a romantic fascination upon English writers for many years to come—upon Thomas Malory, Edmund Spenser, John Milton, and Alfred, Lord Tennyson, to take four of the outstanding examples.

Along with the Arthurian romances, there came into England a number of popular tales, some of them based on Byzantine and classical stories, others of more complex origin. Though they were written in French, the heroes of some of them—Guy of Warwick and Bevis of Hampton, for example—became English folk-heroes and, later on, the English vernacular versions of these tales were to have a tremendous popular appeal.

During the next stage translations from the French became more and more frequent, as the Normans became increasingly aware of their 'Englishness', and in the process many of them took on a recognizable 'English' character. The loss of Normandy itself during the reign of King John precipitated the process, and from then on English gradually began to replace French, both in official matters and in literature, so that by 1384 an Anglo-Norman writer was able to write that 'now children of the grammar-schools know no more French than their left heels'.

Under these circumstances it was not surprising perhaps that there should be a revival of vernacular literature. There had indeed been a portent of it as early as the beginning of the thirteenth century, when *The Owl and the Nightingale* was composed—a poem of considerable merit, and prophetic of the future English genius for dramatic dialogue. Lyric poetry too began to make its appearance, strongly influenced by French metrical forms but national in character, and, from the middle of the thirteenth century onwards, political songs (usually satirical in nature) were written, as well as battle poems (celebrating the victories of Edward III, for example) some of which recalled the Anglo-Saxon war songs. About the same time patriotic poetry was also being composed in Scotland, notably in praise of Robert the Bruce. Carols—at this date the term does not necessarily imply a connexion with Christmas—and later on ballads also began to make their appearance in increasing numbers.

Prose too received a considerable impetus when John Wyclif, the religious reformer, and his followers (known as the Lollards) sought popular support by writing pamphlets in the vernacular. They also translated parts of the Bible, and though the English style was stiff and clumsy the importance of this beginning of a Biblical tradition in English prose can hardly be exaggerated.

A more dramatic and at first sight surprising phenomenon was a resurgence of the old alliterative verse, at the very moment when Chaucer was beginning to revolutionize English prosody. Some of these alliterative poems were in fact considerably influenced by French poetry and they contain a number of words of French derivation; but most of them are as difficult for the modern reader as *Beowulf* itself—and all of them display the epic swing and beat of the old Anglo-Saxon poems as well as the kind of synonyms and picture-epithets that naturally go with alliterative verse.

Two of them must be singled out for special mention. *Sir Gawayne and the Grene Knight*, yet another addition to Arthurian literature, was composed in the North-Midlands dialect about the year 1360. The story is very ancient and almost certainly of Celtic origin and the poem, besides being a work of original genius, shows how many of the elements of the old pagan religions, both ancient British and Scandinavian, were assimilated into our culture: for the knights and their antagonists in this (as in other Arthurian poems) are descended from the gods and evil spirits of the old mythologies, and their ladies from the Spring or Earth Goddesses. At the same time, in remodelling the Arthurian story so that it would serve as a pattern for courtly and Christian virtue, the anonymous poet of *Sir Gawayne* was a precursor of Spenser in the Arthurian parts of his great poem *The Faerie Queene*.

The other outstanding work of this alliterative renaissance was the composite poem known as *The Vision concerning Piers Plowman*, written by William Langland in the dialect of the West Midlands and existing in a number of manuscripts embodying three principal versions written probably between 1360 and 1399. The starting-point of the poem is a dream, a device borrowed from the same continental French poets who inspired Chaucer in his earlier work, and there are other signs of French influence. But the poet was also a poor priest who lived in close contact with his flock and, in *The Vision concerning Piers Plowman*, we hear for the first time the authentic voice of the ordinary people of England. Langland's passionate attacks on the abuses of the day relate him both to the leaders of the contemporary peasants' revolts (though Langland himself was more visionary than revolutionary) and to that radical, nonconformist strain in the English temperament (often combined with mysticism) that was to contribute so much to our culture. He has in consequence something in common with later writers such as Bunyan, Wesley, and Blake. The similarity in Bunyan's case is particularly striking, for the beginning of Langland's poem— where a vast 'field full of folk' (to quote in modern English) go about their worldly concerns greedily and selfishly, until they are stirred into repentance and set off to discover the sanctuary of Truth—inevitably reminds us of *The Pilgrim's Progress*.

Next to its use of alliterative verse, the allegorical framework is the outstanding characteristic of the poem. Allegory of course was a natural faculty of the medieval mind. It was the means whereby the abstract was made concrete and all kinds of dimly apprehended thoughts and feelings were rendered tangible and visible to the mind's eye. In one form or another, indeed, allegory was to survive far beyond the Middle Ages—not only in the writers already mentioned in connexion with Langland, and in Elizabethans like Spenser—but also in the eighteenth century with writers such as Swift, in the nineteenth century with Samuel Butler—the author of *Erewhon*—and by others, and in more recent times there has been the example of George Orwell.

The vividness and realism of the best parts of Langland's allegory spring above all, however, from its close contact with the popular mind and with the great medieval tradition of preaching. Throughout the whole of this period the clergy were addressing their sermons to the people in the vernacular (it is here perhaps that the submerged Anglo-Saxon spirit lived on most vigorously) and in doing so they naturally used the kinds of homely illustration and turns of speech with which their congregations were familiar in their day-to-day lives.

The section of *Piers Plowman* that comes closest to popular preaching is that dealing with the Seven Deadly Sins. In fact, these grotesque allegorical portraits probably derive from the figures in some pre-Christian ritual, but they had been taken over by the medieval preachers and, through their sermons, passed into the poetry and drama of the Middle Ages. In *Piers Plowman* they are depicted with extraordinary gusto and in them we see the originals of a whole line of English comic characters. The most easily recognizable descendants are in those writings which specialize in caricature—as in the comedies of Ben Jonson in the seventeenth century, and in the novels of Charles Dickens in the nineteenth. But they also contributed to the more 'rounded' comic characters of our literature, including those of Shakespeare.

It would be quite wrong to regard these alliterative poems as isolated freaks. It must be remembered that the life of a manuscript was very precarious at this time; Caxton did not begin printing (in Bruges) until 1474, and in all probability those poems that have survived were not the only ones to be written, quite apart from the fact that there may have been many more never committed to parchment but memorized by the minstrels. That accidental survivals should be of such high quality suggests that a flourishing tradition of alliterative poetry must have persisted in the West Midlands and in North-west England, culminating in what is really the first flowering period of English literature. In one sense, therefore, Chaucer can be regarded as coming at the end of a period rather than at the beginning.

In order to reach a true appreciation of Geoffrey Chaucer's originality and genius, it is necessary to understand his indebtedness to the past. Behind his work lay centuries of oral and written practice in several languages—and by no means the least important of these was English itself. It is true that his main literary influences were continental, but he was well acquainted with Anglo-Saxon literature, including the contemporary alliterative poems, and, what is more to the point, every fibre of his poetic being was soaked in the idiom of everyday English usage, at all levels of society. Indeed he probably owed more to the English he heard spoken around him than he did to the French and Italian poets.

In spite of his apparent 'modernity', Chaucer was firmly rooted in the medieval world, as many of his poems, particularly the early ones, demonstrate. He was, for example, as much addicted to allegory as any of his contemporaries; the concepts of chivalry and of courtly love appear frequently in his work; the Anglo-Saxon device of 'flyting' (the exchange of satirical abuse)

An illustration from *Sir Gawayne and the Grene Knight*, late 14th or early 15th century manuscript

A page from the 15th century Ellesmere Chaucer manuscript

attracted him, and sometimes he combined it with the old animal fable, in somewhat the same way as the Anglo-Saxon poet of *The Owl and the Nightingale*; and he can indulge in as much rambling medieval folk-lore as any.

But he was also thoroughly cosmopolitan. By comparison, poets like Langland, despite their undoubted merits, appear insular and restricted. With Chaucer we feel we have left the cramped confines of the old Anglo-Saxon world.

For the first time England had a great writer who was not only a man of the world but a man of many worlds. In his lifetime Chaucer was page, squire, diplomat, and scholar. He mingled with courtiers, soldiers, city burghers, merchants, and the common folk alike. His imagination was stirred and his vision extended by his travels in France and Italy and by his contact with the spirit of the Early Renaissance. He made full use in his work of his wide reading not only of medieval Latin but also of the Latin classics, particularly Virgil and Ovid, while many of his writings show the impact of French and Italian works; the influence of the *Decamerone* of Boccaccio upon the underlying plan of the *Canterbury Tales* is an outstanding example.

The full force of his originality showed itself above all in the revolutionary changes which he brought about in the language of English literature. At the time he began to write, it was by no means certain which of the various English dialects would become the staple—if indeed there was to be a single literary language at all. It is true that the dialect of the East Midlands had become 'the King's English', the one used by London, the Court, and the Universities. But the fact that these were also the places where French had been most valued meant that there was a considerable prejudice against the use of the vernacular for literary purposes— and it is noteworthy that the output of literature there was far inferior to that in the other regions—and, as we have seen, the great alliterative poems of the period were written in other dialects.

Chaucer, however, staked his whole literary reputation upon the dialect of the East Midlands. At the same time, he abandoned the old alliterative principle (though, of course, in common with all our poets he uses alliteration for emotional and atmospheric effects), substituting for it the prosody of rhyme and number. He imported the decasyllabic line from France, subjected it to Italian influence, and turned it into 'the heroic line'—the vehicle for nearly all our great poetry from this point onwards. He used this new line in a variety of ways hitherto unknown in this country; of these, the seven-line stanza (the so-called 'rhyme royal' which was to be the basis of Spenser's famous stanza) and, even more, the 'heroic couplet' were to be of tremendous import for the future. In Chaucer's hands, in fact, English prosody as we know it was firmly established. Whereas the effect of the old alliterative verse—though it had strengths of its own—was of a repetitive drum-beat, Chaucer's poetry is alive with all kinds of subtle forms, tones, modulations, and rhythmical variations; for the first time real music has entered English poetry.

These new instruments were put to their greatest test in the *Canterbury Tales* in which Chaucer deployed the whole bustling medieval scene, high and low, rich and poor, cleric and lay, good and bad. The famous *Prologue* to the *Tales* is a brilliant cavalcade of a whole age and society. But the people in it are far from being static figures in a frieze: on the contrary they are in perpetual motion, not only in *The Prologue* itself but also in the interludes between the tales, which are themselves chosen and placed for dramatic effect. Thus *The Frere's Tale* is directed against the Somnour, and *The Somnour's Tale* against the Friar, and *The Clerke's Tale* of the patient wife Grisilde is a reply and a rebuke to the Wife of Bath's bawdy and irreverent treatment of the married state. Moreover, although Chaucer never finished the *Canterbury Tales*, an overall dramatic pattern clearly emerges.

In addition, the characters of the *Canterbury Tales* are at one and the same time representatives of their class and status within the society to which they belong, individuals in their own right—and (as Blake was to point out) types of universal significance. The blending of these three aspects makes them 'rounded' figures in marked contrast to the two-dimensional portraits we encounter in *The Vision concerning Piers Plowman*. This advance in the concept of characterization was to have a profound effect both on the drama and eventually on the novel.

In this connexion another of Chaucer's great works must be mentioned. On a superficial level *Troilus and Criseyde* is a tale of courtly love derived from one of Boccaccio's works. But Chaucer turns it into what is virtually the first great English novel—and this statement can be taken quite literally, for not only does it tell a story with all the variation, alternations of light and shade, and amplitude of a great novel, but its analysis of behaviour and motive is as subtle as anything in later fiction. In particular Criseyde is the first detailed study of a woman in

18

English literature, and Pandare is the first really complete comic character.

In comic invention indeed Chaucer was especially prolific. The vitality of the various rogues in the *Canterbury Tales* is inexhaustible, and was to have a profound influence upon the Elizabethan literature of vagabondage and therefore indirectly upon such picaresque eighteenth-century novels as Henry Fielding's *The History of Tom Jones, a Foundling* and Defoe's *Moll Flanders*. Moll also reminds us of the Wife of Bath—one of the greatest of English comic characters, an amazing embodiment of primitive vitality, a kind of female Falstaff—with whom she has a good deal in common.

The great achievements to which Chaucer pointed the way, however, lay a good way ahead. It was two hundred years before England produced a poet worthy to rank beside him. His immediate successors were for the most part also his slavish imitators. They turned, moreover, to his earlier 'literary' phase rather than to the *Canterbury Tales*, and even here they failed to recapture his freshness and gaiety. The nearest to him in spirit was John Gower, though his interminable poem, *Confessio Amantis*, written about 1384, cannot stand comparison with a single one of Chaucer's larger poems. It is however of some interest. Its smooth-flowing but un-impassioned verse looked forward to the kind of writing, half poetry half prose, that was to have a vogue in the eighteenth century. It is also a repository of some of the most popular tales in this age of story-telling, and therefore a link in the development of English fiction. But it is certainly no starting-point in any other way, for it is thoroughly medieval in tone, particularly in its relentless didacticism.

The only true heirs to Chaucer before the sixteenth century were a group of poets known as the Scottish Chaucerians. They wrote in the Northern or Scottish variant of the English tongue ('Inglis', as they called it) and the greatest of them, Robert Henryson, used the Chaucerian stanza to compose a sequel to *Troilus and Criseyde* entitled the *Testament of Cresseid*, a moving and genuinely tragic poem in which Cresseid, abandoned by her lover, contracts leprosy. Henryson was also a worthy follower of Chaucer in his fresh and vivid the *Morall Fabillis of Esope the Phrygian*. The Scottish Chaucerians as a whole can be seen as the forerunners of a long line of Scots poets, a line that passes through Burns and Scott in the eighteenth century and continues right through to twentieth-century Scots poets such as Hugh McDiarmid.

English Literature

As far as England was concerned, however, there was more real poetry in the traditional ballads than in the more formal works. These were short, vivid narratives closely related to folk-lore, meant to be sung (and probably danced as well) and for the most part transmitted orally. Though only a few of them can with certainty be placed before the Renaissance—perhaps only *The Nut Brown Maid* and the *Ballad of Chevy Chase*—a large number of them were almost certainly in circulation in the fourteenth and fifteenth centuries. The quintessential poetic spell of these simple poems is proved by the way in which, time after time, they have revivified jaded literary tastes, in particular towards the end of the Age of Reason when they became one of the factors in the Romantic Revival.

The record of English prose in the fifteenth century is in the main one of retrogression by way of revolution. For although it was in 1476 that William Caxton (himself a prose writer and translator) established the first printing press in England—an event which was, of course, to have tremendous repercussions—paradoxically its immediate effect, far from leading on to a new age, was to bolster up the medieval way of life. Most of the books that came from his press were translations of earlier medieval works, among them versions of old French romances. One of these derived from French sources was to become one of the classics of our literature—the *Morte d'Arthure* of Sir Thomas Malory.

This book is yet another proof of the persistency of the Arthurian *mystique*. It is, however, nothing like as bold and energetic an interpretation of it as the earlier *Sir Gawayne and the Grene Knight*. Malory's approach is almost self-indulgently nostalgic and the work has a decided *fin de siècle* atmosphere. His prose style, too, beautiful though it is in many respects, is studied in its effects, especially in the deliberate use of archaisms. The *Morte d'Arthure* has a considerable influence upon later writers (not always a happy one, as it tended to produce preciosity) including Spenser and many years later Lord Tennyson, who drew upon it for the composition of his *Idylls of the King*.

Apart, however, from a few learned works which showed the language struggling to adapt itself as a medium for discussion and exposition, and the *Paston Letters* (not meant of course for publication) which give us some vivid glimpses into the daily life of a typical well-to-do middle-class family of the fifteenth century and which look forward to a later era of prolific diary and letter writing,

brought With hym Phelip his brothers doughter that Was erle of
henaute his nece in to englond / & kyng edward spoused hir at yorke
With moch honour ¶ And sir Johan of Bothum Bisshop of Ely
& sir William of Melton Erchebisshop of yorke songen the masse p
sonday in the eue of conuersion of seint Paule In the yere of grace
a.M.CC.xxviij. But for enchesen that the kyng Was but yong & ten
dre of age / Whan he Was crouned full many Wronges Were done Whi
le that his fadre lyued / for enchesen that he trowed the Counselers
that Were fals aboute hym that counseilled hym to done othir Wyse
than reson Wolde / Wherfor grete harme Was do Un to the Reame &
to the kyng & all men directed it the kynges dede / & it Was not so Al
myghty god Woke / Wherfor it Was ordeyned at the kynges crounyng
that the kyng for his tendre age shold be gouerned by xij .grete
lordes of eglond Withoute Which no thyng shold be done / that is for
to say The Erchebisshop of Caunterbury / the erchebisshop o yorke
The Bisshop of Wynchestre / & the Bisshop of hereford / the Erle of la
castre / the erle marchall / & the Erle of kent that Were the kynges
Uncles / & the erle of Garenne / Sir Thomas Wake / Sir Henry of
Percy / Sir Oliuer of yngham and Johan of Roos barons /
¶ All these Were sworne treWly for to counseill the kyng ¶ And
they shold ansuere euery yere in the parlement of that that sholde be
done in the tyme of that gouernaille But that ordinaunce Was sone
Undone / & that Was moch losse & harme to all englond For p kyng
and all the lordes that shold gouerne hym Were gouerned & ruled
after the kynges moder Dame Isabell / & by Sir Rogier Mortimer
And as they Wolde all thyng Was done both amonge high & loWe
And they token Un to hem Castelles tounes landes & rentes in gre
te harme & losse to the crowne & of the kynges state oute of mesure

¶ HoW the pees Was made BitWene the Englisshmen and the scot
tes / and also of Justisyng of TrypleBastone
Capitulo ducentesimo xvij.

He kyng EdWard at Witsontyde the second yere of his re
gne thurgh counseill of his moder & of sir Rogier Morti
mer ordeyned a plement at northampton / at the Which ple
ment the kyng thurgh hir counseill & none othir of the land Within
age graunted to bene acorded With the scottes in this maner / that
all the feautes & homages that the scottes shold do Un to the croune
of englond forgafe hem Un to the scottes for eu more by his chartre

Caxton presenting the *Recuyell of the Historyes of Troye* to Margaret of York. Anonymous woodcut, *c.* 1475

English prose gave little indication at this stage that the English Renaissance was on its way.

The really significant developments in the period between the death of Chaucer and the Renaissance were in the field of popular drama. The distant origins lie in the ancient pagan rituals, in the recitations of the Anglo-Saxon 'scop' and his descendant the minstrel, and possibly in theatrical performances introduced into Britain by the Romans during their occupation. But the immediate source was those parts of the Christian rituals which contained dramatic elements, notably the services at Easter and Christmas and possibly the Mass itself. Various liturgical dramas appear to have grown out of these services and gradually these drew away from the church and its precincts until, some time between the thirteenth and fourteenth centuries, they became completely secularized. They were no longer spoken in Latin but in the vernacular. Instead of brief liturgical speeches whole dramatic scripts were devised, and these were extended to cover a wide range of biblical stories. And the actors were no longer clergy but members of the medieval guilds who, for certain feast days, particularly for the festival of Corpus Christi in June, prepared a whole series of these biblical plays, each guild being responsible for one play. The plays would be mounted on platforms with wheels so that they could be drawn from one 'station' to another. The whole cycle would represent the Christian 'History of Man' from the Creation to the Last Judgment.

Four of these cycles have been preserved in manuscripts of the fifteenth century and later, though they had probably assumed the form in which we find them earlier than this. Crude though the plays are in many respects they display flashes of poetry and elements of genuine comedy and tragic pathos. Moreover they contain in embryo many of the character-types, themes, and conventions of Elizabethan drama. For example, the Herod and Pilate of the Mystery Plays are braggarts and ranters of the kind to be met with in many Elizabethan and Jacobean comedies. Abraham's grief when he is called upon to sacrifice Isaac was echoed in several Elizabethan plays where parents mourn over their children: while Noah's wife is the prototype of many of the 'scolds' of Elizabethan drama including Katharina in Shakespeare's *The Taming of the Shrew*.

The Miracle Plays, too, by introducing ordinary characters side by side with biblical figures, saints, and angels, anticipated the

English Literature

Elizabethan practice of mixing different social levels and the natural with the supernatural in their plays. And most important of all perhaps was the association in several of them of buffoonery with the profoundest issues of life and death. Thus, in the Christmas play of the Towneley Cycle, the birth of Christ is attended by an episode in which a sheep-stealer dresses up a stolen sheep as a baby and hides it in a cradle where it is discovered by the shepherds who are shortly to be summoned by the angels to the crib of the infant Christ. In juxtapositions such as these are to be found the origins of that blending of comedy and tragedy which was to be one of the chief and most effective characteristics of the great age of our drama. It may seem a long step from the buffoons of the Miracle Plays to Lear's tragic Fool. Nevertheless they belong to the same family.

2 · The Renaissance in England

IT is difficult to see the earlier part of our literature as a coherent whole. Broken up by the effects of successive invasions, it is a story of fits and starts; like the moon it shines brightly one moment, to be blotted out by storm-clouds the next, and only with the advent of Chaucer does it begin to ride high and free.

The period discussed in this chapter is perhaps even more complex. But underlying it are two unifying principles—the great revolution in European man's intellectual and spiritual outlook, known as the Renaissance, and the equally far-reaching religious reorientation which we call the Reformation.

One of the first symptoms of the new attitudes was a widespread questioning of scholasticism, the theological and philosophical system created by various Christian thinkers, notably St Thomas Aquinas, and based upon an authoritarian interpretation of the works of the ancient Greek philosopher Aristotle. For years this system had seemed fixed and inviolable, so much so that any new idea or theory, no matter how much empirical proof supported it, was in danger of suppression by the Church authorities if it could not be readily fitted into it.

The men who challenged this system are known as the humanists —because they were interested in man himself rather than in his relation to a fixed order of things. They found their inspiration in the classics of antiquity, and particularly in those of ancient Greece. This revival of classical learning began in Italy as early as the fourteenth century, but there was a period, roughly between 1490 and 1520, when English scholars were in the van of the humanist movement. Some of them, who had travelled in Italy where they had studied classical manuscripts, established brilliant schools of Greek at the Universities and at St Paul's School which was founded by one of their number, Dean John Colet. The greatest of them was Sir Thomas More, the first Englishman since Bede to achieve any considerable international reputation.

More's famous *Utopia*, written in Latin about 1515, was in many respects a typical humanist document. It poked fun at scholasticism and at the medieval concepts of chivalry, turned to the influence of Plato (whose *Republic* was one of its main inspirations), and asserted the superiority of Greek over Latin.

There were, however, special factors affecting the course of the Renaissance in England. First and foremost was the peculiarly nationalistic shape the Reformation assumed. Henry VIII's quarrel with the Pope over the divorce question, followed by the Act of Supremacy and the first steps that led to the establishment of the Church of England, inevitably altered the whole balance of political and religious life, and therefore the balance of literature, art, and thought. Two immediate consequences were that Henry's dissolution of the monasteries struck a considerable blow at the new classical learning (though it also helped to hasten the abandonment of scholasticism) and that the work of Sir Thomas More, who was beheaded for his opposition to the King's break with Rome, was for the time being discredited.

For while the humanists looked to classical antiquity for a moral and intellectual revival, the Protestant reformers insisted that salvation could be found only in the Scriptures. Thus the Renaissance in England was less 'pagan' and more thoroughly imbued with religious thought and feeling than in some other countries, and the fact that in England there was no strong tradition in the plastic arts and therefore no possibility of the kind of creative upsurge in sculpture and painting that constituted the chief glory of Renaissance Italy, also helped to drive the new emotions and energies inwards to the levels of spirit and conscience.

One of the most important results was a fresh impetus towards the translation of the Bible, already initiated, as we have seen, by Wyclif and his followers. Although the 'pestilential glosses' which accompanied William Tyndale's translation of the New Testament had earned the disapproval of Henry VIII in his earlier role as Defender of the Faith, Tyndale's Bible, completed by Miles Coverdale in 1535, was soon accepted throughout the country, and was to be the basis for the even more famous Authorized Version of 1611—the work of forty-seven scholars which, at the King's command, became the official Bible of the Church of England.

Almost as important as the Bible of Tyndale and Coverdale was the *Book of Common Prayer*, an anonymous compilation from the Latin missal published under the direction of Archbishop Cranmer in 1549. The language of these two great translations, vivid, lucid, and dignified, speaking to all classes and listened to by all classes, was a tremendously potent influence upon our literature.

There was one other work, typical of the Protestant partisan writing of the period, which was as widely read, both at this time and later, as the Bible itself. This was *Acts and Monuments of these latter and perilous Dayes, touching matters of the Church, wherein are comprehended and described the great Persecutions and horrible Troubles that have been wrought and practised by the Romishe Prelates, especiallye in this Realm of England and Scotlande, from the yeare of our Lorde a Thousande unto the Tyme now present. Gathered and collected according to the true copies and wrytings certificatorie, as wel of the Parties themselves that suffered, as also out of the Bishops' Registers which were the doers thereof, by John Foxe* (in Latin 1559, in English 1563), better known to later generations as the *Book of Martyrs*.

There is another aspect of humanism in England that must be noted. The early Tudor monarchs, in their policy of breaking up the old feudal aristocracy, needed a new and better educated class of administrators—and as Sir Thomas Elyot pointed out in his *Boke of the Governour* in 1531—the new classical learning provided an excellent training-ground for them. It is here that we have the beginnings of that close contact between the court and the world of learning and literature that was such an outstanding feature of the reign of Elizabeth I. By Shakespeare's lifetime, accomplishment in language and the arts was not merely a matter of personal pleasure but also an important means of advancement. This was true not only of the new class of poor professional writers and of emergent country gentlemen like Shakespeare but also of the great nobles whose lands had been impoverished by the policies of Henry VII and Henry VIII and who were increasingly dependent upon the court. The Renaissance in England therefore was to a considerable degree involved with the consolidation of the Tudor régime itself.

Although humanism came to England quite early her literary development was slow in the extreme. Even the language, since the death of Chaucer, had lapsed into a state of confusion, whereas the native tongues of Italy, France, Spain, and other continental countries had long since matured into instruments fully capable of expressing the excitements and inspirations of the Renaissance. This confusion affected prose as well as poetry and it is significant that the two landmarks that stand at either end of the humanist movement in England—Sir Thomas More's *Utopia* and Sir Francis Bacon's *Instauratio Magna*—were both written in Latin.

The tally of English prose works in the early Tudor period

would, however, have been even more disappointing but for Sir Thomas More. For it was in English that, in 1513, he wrote his *History of the Life and Death of King Edward V and of the usurpation of Richard III* which does not merely describe events in the manner of most of the contemporary chroniclers, but—admittedly in a partisan spirit—selects, marshals, and interprets them. He bases his findings, moreover, upon a searching estimate of character, and Shakespeare was to draw substantially upon this work when he came to write his play on the same theme.

Two other early Tudor works also provided material for Shakespeare: Edward Hall's *Union of the Two Noble and Illustre famelies of Lancastre and Yorke*, commonly known as Hall's *Chronicle* (1548), which dealt with the Wars of the Roses and the reigns of the first two Tudor monarchs, and Sir John Cheke's *The Heart of Sedicion, how grievous it is to a Communewelth*, which was directed against the Norfolk rebels and which contained sentiments about mob rule which were to be echoed half a century later in the famous scene in *Coriolanus* where Menenius castigates the Roman populace. The more influential chronicles of Raphael Holinshed were not published until 1577.

A few other prose writers, such as the humanist Roger Ascham in *Toxophilus, the schole of shootinge contaynd in two bookes*, a book devoted to archery, and in *The Scholemaster* (published in 1570, two years after his death) possessed a certain pungency of style. And some of them were well aware that the English language was sadly in need of discipline: Sir Thomas Wilson, for example, in his *Arte of Rhetorique for the use of all suche as are studious of eloquence sette forth in English* (1553) advocated (and occasionally practised) 'purity' of style, and the avoidance of 'inkhorn termes' and 'outlandish Englische'.

On the whole, however, translations from foreign prose writers were more important at this stage than original works. Outstanding among these—at any rate as far as future influence was concerned—were Thomas Hoby's translation of Castiglione's *Il Cortegiano* in 1561, and Sir Thomas North's rendering in 1579 (from a French version) of the *Vitae Parallellae* of the ancient Greek biographer Plutarch—upon which Shakespeare drew heavily for his Roman plays. It must not be forgotten, either, that there was a good deal of popular writing during this period. The French romances, for example, continued to enjoy the vogue they had won in the Middle Ages in spite of the disapproval of the Protestants. Various collections of stories also enjoyed a wide audience, and the Jest Books, especially those which provided a loose thread to the various items by assigning them to an imaginary or real person (as in *Tarleton's Jests*) formed a link with the picaresque writings of the later Elizabethans and thus with the great picaresque novels of the eighteenth century.

And, of course, behind all the disquisitions of the theorists and all the attempts of learned gentlemen to elevate the language lay the vivid, racy English of the countryside and the market place—that 'language really used by men', to borrow Wordsworth's phrase, which must nourish the roots of any literature that is to be truly a living one. At this stage however it was chiefly the preachers in their sermons—and notably Bishop Latimer, the farmer's son—who showed most awareness of these largely untapped resources.

At first poetry was even more backward than prose. That progress was made at all was almost entirely due to the work of two men—Sir Thomas Wyatt and Henry Howard, Earl of Surrey—and they had practically to start from scratch, so degenerate had English versification become since the death of Chaucer.

Chaucer indeed was one of Wyatt's chief inspirations. Like him, Wyatt travelled in Italy, was deeply influenced by the Italian poets, and borrowed from them verse-forms hitherto unknown to his fellow-countrymen. The most important of these was the sonnet, as practised by the fourteenth-century Italian poet Petrarch, which brought both lyricism and discipline back into English poetry. Equally important was the quality of personal impassioned utterance in Wyatt's sonnets and songs alike—a quality which had been heard but rarely since Chaucer.

The Earl of Surrey, Wyatt's younger contemporary and admirer, by smoothing out many of the irregularities and rough edges which still remained in Wyatt, carried English versification yet closer to the great Elizabethan flowering. In addition he introduced a new kind of sonnet, whereby for the Petrarchan arrangement of two quatrains followed by two tercets he substituted the form of three quatrains with different rhymes resting upon a final couplet. The Petrarchan sonnet was to have an honourable future, but it was the more flexible form introduced by Surrey that Shakespeare used, and after him many of our greatest poets.

Even more momentous was the introduction by Surrey of blank verse, which he used, with considerable effect, for his translation, about 1541, of the second and fourth books of Virgil's *Aeneid*. Both

Wyatt and Surrey, then, showed how English verse could recover some of the ground lost since Chaucer. But it was not until 1557, when both of them were dead, that any of their poems appeared in print, in a collection made by a London publisher named Richard Tottel. And although *Tottel's Miscellany* (as it was commonly known) is undoubtedly a landmark in the history of English poetry, and although it contained a few other fine poems (by Thomas, Lord Vaux, for example) the collections that followed, in spite of such attractive titles as *The Paradise of Dainty Devices*, *A Gorgious Gallery of Gallant Inventions*, and *A Posie of Gillowflowers* contained no verse of outstanding merit and no real growing-points. For the time being it seemed that Wyatt and Surrey were men born out of their time.

The main reason behind this slowness of development in English literature was the strength and persistency of popular habits of speech, thought, and entertainment rooted in the communal life of towns and villages which were still largely medieval. We have already seen these forces at work in the case of prose. But it was in drama that they were particularly powerful.

It is true that the cycles of Miracle Plays slowly died out during the sixteenth century. This was not due to any lack of popular support but to the opposition of the Protestant clergy and authorities—who thought they encouraged too much ribaldry and probably distrusted them as the products of the deposed Church—and the guilds fought hard to keep them. Gradually, however, the Morality Plays—in which the characters were abstract vices and virtues—began to rival the popularity of the Miracle Plays.

These Morality Plays were, of course, close to the medieval tradition, particularly in their allegorical structure; in some cases these were actively sponsored by the clergy and they were certainly designed to further the ends of Christianity. But as time went on they also served both as vehicles for the new humanist ideas and for furthering specifically Protestant doctrines. Thus a Morality called *The Play of Wyt and Science* was pervaded by the humanist faith in learning and reason, while Sir David Lindesay's *Ane Satyre of the Thrie Estaits* which was first played in 1540, was one of the masterpieces of the Reformation in Scotland, and in England Bishop Bale also put Moralities to Protestant uses.

One of these has a special place in the history of our drama, for in *King Jehan* Bale, turning the historical King John into a Protestant hero because of his quarrel with the Pope, introduced

28

☙ The proude primacie of

Popes paynted out in Tables, in order of
their rifyng vp by little and little, from
faythful Byfhops and Martyrs, to become Lords
and gouernours ouer Kyng and kyngdomes,
exalting themfelues in the Temple of
God, aboue all that is called
God. &c. 2. Theffal. 2.

Pfalmes and Hymnes together. In all which their dreadfull daungers, and forowfull afflictions, notwithftandyng the goodnes of the Lord left them not defolate: but the more their outward tribulations did increafe, the more their inward confolations did abound: and the farther of they feemed from the ioyes of this lyfe, the more prefent was the Lord with them with grace and fortitude to confirme and retiofte their foules. And though their poffeffions and riches in this world were loft and fpoyled: yet were they enriched with heauely giftes and treafures from aboue an hundreth fold. Then was true Religion truely fett in hart. Then was Chaftianitie not in outward appearaunce fhewed, but in inward affection receiued, and the true image of the Church not in outwrab fhew pretenfed, but in her perfect ftate effectuall. Then was the name and feare of God true in hart, not in lyppes alone wordlyng. Fayth then was feruent, zeale ardent, prayer not beginnyng in the lippes, but groned out to God from the bottome of the fpirite. Then was no pride in the Church, nor lapfure to feeke riches, nor tyme to keepe them. Contention for trifles was then fo far fro Chriftians, that well were they when they could meete to pray together agaynft the deuill, authour of all diffention. Brefly the whole Churche of Chrift Iefus with all the members therof, the farther it was from the type and fhape of this world, the nearer it was to the blefled refpect of Gods fauour and fupportation.

The true riches of the church defcribed.

❡ The firft rifing of the Byfhops of Rome.

A Fter this long tyme of trouble, it pleafed the Lord at length mercyfully to looke vpon the Saintes and feruauntes of his fonne, to releafe their captiuitie, to releafe their miferie, and to bynde vp the old Dragon the Deuill, which fo long vexed them, wherby the Church began to afpire to fome more libertie: and the Byfhops which before were as abiectes, vtterly in contempt of Emperours, through the prouidence of God (which difpofeth all thynges in hys tyme after his owne will) began now of Emperours to be efteemed and had in price. Furthermore, as Emperours grew

The firft rifing of the Byfhops of Rome.

The martyrdom of good byfhops vnder wicked Emperours in the primitive Church.

I F the Table of the primitiue Church aboue defcribed, hath bene (gentle reader) fet forth and exhibited before thine eyes the greuious afflictions and forowfull tormentes, which tharough Gods fecret fufferaunce, fell vpon the true Saintes and members of Chriftes Churche in that tyme, efpecially vpon the good Byfhops, Minifters, and teachers of the flocke: of whom fome were fcourged, fome beheaded, fome crucified, fome burned, fome had their eyes put out, fome one way fome an other miferably confumed: which dayes of wofull calamitie continued (as is tofore fhewed) neare the fpace of CCC. yeares. During which tyme the deare fpoufe & elect Church of God, beyng fharply affaulted on euery fide, had fmall reft, no ioy, nor outward fafety in this prefent world, but in much bitternes of hart, in continuall teares and mournyng vnder the croffe paffed ouer their dayes, beyng fpoyled, imprifoned, contemned, reuiled, famifhed, flaundred and Martyred euery where. Who neither durft well tary at home for feare and dread: & much leffe durft come abroad for the enemyes, but onely by night, When they affembled as they might, fometymes to fing

Here begynneth a treatyse how the
hye fader of heuen sendeth dethe
to somon euery creature to
come and gyue a counte
of theyr lyues in this
worlde and is in ma-
ner of a morall
playe.

Everyman and Death; the title-page woodcut from a 16th century edition
of *Everyman*

real and allegorical characters side by side, so that the piece is both a Morality and an embryonic history play—one in fact which has distant affinities with Shakespeare's play on the same subject.

Not that the allegorical characters in the Moralities are themselves deficient in dramatic force. Often they have a vivid life of their own, recalling the portraits of the Seven Deadly Sins in Langland's *Piers Plowman,* while the opposition of Good and Evil frequently produced genuine dramatic conflict. The popularity of *Everyman* (derived from a Dutch original) even today bears witness to the intrinsic vigour of these plays. Incidentally many of them contained low comedy relief of the type introduced into the Towneley Miracle Play about the shepherds, and in the early stages at any rate the Moralities probably appealed to the same kind of public as the Miracle Plays.

Interludes, on the other hand, were at first intended for performance in the houses of the more learned Tudor gentry and the name probably derives from the fact they were presented in the intervals between other entertainments. The best known (of those that have survived) are four farcical plays by John Heywood, probably derived from French *fabliaux,* which although they consist chiefly of dialogues also contain some vivid and witty passages and at least the rudiments of character and plot.

From about the middle of the fifteenth century developments in the drama came thick and fast. First and foremost there was the formation of troupes of professional players to meet the increasing demand, in the provinces as well as in the capital, for dramatic entertainments of all kinds, including the more farcical of the Interludes—a demand which could no longer be satisfied by the amateur performances of the Miracle Plays or by the cruder semi-dramatic entertainment known as 'Jigs'.

The strolling players in the provinces, harried by the authorities as vagabonds, soon found it necessary to place themselves under the protection of some interested nobleman—and the first company to obtain letters patent was that of the Duke of Leicester in 1574. In London the players were protected from the civic authorities—particularly hostile when Puritans (the word 'Puritan' began to be applied about 1564)—by the Privy Council, acting on behalf of the Crown. At first they played in the courtyards of inns but, as they were still subjected to many interferences, in 1576 the first professional theatre was built outside the city boundaries at Shoreditch—to be followed at intervals by others until by the end of the century there were about eight of them.

English Literature

Needless to say the creation of an acting profession and the building of theatres for it to operate in were powerful factors in the evolution of a national drama.

At the same time plays began to be performed by the barristers at the Inns of Court, by the boy choristers of the Chapel Royal, and soon by the pupils of various London schools—much to the disgust, of course, of the professional players. Although in many cases these were played to popular audiences as well as to the Court—for whom they were primarily intended—they were usually of a more scholarly nature, and it was in these theatres that the influences of classical drama began to make themselves felt.

It was indeed a headmaster of Westminster School, Nicholas Udall, who in 1533 wrote *Ralph Roister Doister* for his pupils to perform. Many of the characters were borrowed from the Latin playwright Plautus, but they also have abundant life of their own and the play is in fact the first thorough-going English comedy. In addition it contains songs, a mock dirge, rustic clowns, and many other ingredients that were to go to the making of mature Elizabethan comedy. At about the same time another farce, *Gammer Gurton's Needle* (probably by William Stevenson) was performed at Christ's College, Cambridge. This takes from Latin comedy only the distribution into acts and the regular structure: for the rest it is boisterous and realistic comedy and it contains a fine drinking song.

It was the fact that the classical model could be grafted on to a strong native tradition of comedy that saved plays such as these from becoming mere academic exercises. In the case of tragedy, on the other hand, there was no comparable native tradition. The playwrights at this stage, moreover, turned not to the great tragedies of ancient Greece, which were little known throughout the Renaissance (in spite of the humanists) and very rarely translated, but to Seneca, a highly didactic Roman philosopher (died in A.D. 65) who wrote equally didactic tragedies.

These were derived from the same mythological stories that had been used by Aeschylus, Sophocles, and Euripides, but for their religious concept of destiny and retribution Seneca substituted the motive of human revenge. His plots, full of horror and bloodshed, were conducted mostly off-stage and retailed by the classical device of messengers, so that while there was no direct action, no dramatic movement, and no development of character, there was only too ample a scope for long rhetorical speeches in which Seneca could indulge his taste for moralizing. What is more, it is doubtful whether these plays had ever been staged in Seneca's day, in the real sense of the word: they were fundamentally chamber-plays, to be declaimed rather than acted.

There was therefore a distinct danger that the influence of Seneca might have turned English tragedy into a series of academic exercises. Fortunately his plays, besides providing some timely lessons in discipline and structure, also contained elements that corresponded to popular tastes and traditions. His fondness for violence and atrocities certainly found a ready response, while the public that delighted in the rant and rhetoric of the Herod of the Miracle Plays had no difficulty in accustoming themselves to the same qualities in Senecan drama. Even the long sententious speeches which make the plays of Seneca and his English followers such dull reading for us today could be stomached by a public already trained through the Moralities to accept a good deal of moral discourse.

There can, at any rate, be no doubt as to Seneca's popularity. All his tragedies were translated into English, and most of them were probably performed, between 1559 and 1581. Their influence was immediate and lasting. As early as 1562 a tragedy by Thomas Sackville, Earl of Dorset, and Sir Thomas Norton, written on the Senecan model and entitled *The Tragedie of Gorboduc*, was performed at the Inns of Court. It has most of the faults of its model, including dullness, but it was also a landmark in the history of English drama. For this was the first genuine English tragedy, and also the first English play to be written entirely in blank verse. Its main theme, the dangers that follow an unsettled succession, had a strong topical interest; it had dignity and occasionally nobility of utterance, and it contained some of the seeds of future achievements.

During the twenty years or so that followed the production of *Gorboduc* the ever-growing popular demand for dramatic entertainment was met by a number of translations and adaptations of Italian and Dutch plays, by a number of 'chronicle' or history plays, and by several native tragedies, of which *Cambyses* in 1569 (probably by Thomas Preston) was the most significant. Like the earlier *King Jehan* of Bishop Bale, it mingled real and allegorical characters, and was also clearly influenced in method by the Miracle Plays. But at the same time it bears witness to humanist learning, reveals Seneca's influence, succeeds in drawing a complex and lifelike hero, and mixes tragedy and buffoonery. Here in fact is a play that, in spite of its crudity of style, already contains nearly all the separate elements that went to the making of the great Elizabethan tragedies—except the genius needed to fuse them together.

But in discussing the origins of Elizabethan drama it is essential to remember that it was popular demand that gave genius, when at last it manifested itself, its opportunities. Although it became fashionable among Elizabethan playwrights, including Shakespeare, to decry popular tastes, the emergence of a great national drama would not have been possible without the support of the 'groundlings'.

It was in fact fortunate for English literature from several points of view that popular customs and traditions proved so tenacious. For, although they had been chiefly responsible for holding back the full flowering of the Renaissance in England, they ensured that when it did come it was firmly rooted in rich and vigorous soil.

Moreover the delay itself had advantages. It meant that English literature was simultaneously enriched by the new classical learning and by the matured products of the more precocious European literatures. It meant too that the full force of the Renaissance struck at the very moment when the Counter-Reformation was gathering momentum on the Continent and the English Church and State were in imminent danger, so that the creative outburst coincided with an upsurge of patriotic and Protestant fervour which further strengthened and deepened it.

It is indeed astonishing how suddenly the literary scene was transformed. When Sir Philip Sidney wrote his *Defence of Poesie* in 1583 he could point to little in the way of positive achievement to justify his hopes for the future of English literature. And yet, within little more than twenty years, England had passed through the greatest period in her literary history and had produced work that is amongst the greatest the world has ever known.

Even so, as far as poetry was concerned, the first real genius produced by the English Renaissance was something of a freak case. It is true of course that in *The Shepheardes Calender*, published in 1579, Edmund Spenser at last brought English versification back to the level attained by Chaucer, 'the well of English undefiled' as Spenser calls him, and his acknowledged master. In Spenser's poem the roughnesses and uncertainties that had still to some extent marred the poetry of Wyatt and Surrey have been completely eliminated, and the musical virtuosity and variety are almost as astonishing as in Chaucer himself.

At the same time *The Shepheardes Calender* contains a considerable number of archaic words and expressions (many of them in fact borrowed from Chaucer) and though these delighted Spenser's contemporary readers they were really alien to their experience. Spenser's attachment to the past was, in fact, to some degree nostalgic and retrogressive and his work was not really in the mainstream of the English tradition.

This is true even of his great unfinished poem *The Faerie Queene*, where the astonishing virtuosity that had evinced itself in *The Shepheardes Calender* was applied with 'high seriousness' to a task of epic dimensions. It is of course a landmark in English literary history, the first full-scale poetic masterpiece since the *Canterbury Tales*, and one of which the Elizabethans were justly proud, boasting that it was worthy to stand beside the great epics of antiquity and that it far surpassed the *Orlando Furioso* of Ariosto, one of the works it set out to challenge. There were many respects, too, in which it was a typical Renaissance work. It embodied most of the ideas of the period and it was a treasure-house of echoes and reminiscences from the classics and from the poets of Renaissance France and Italy. It was also a genuinely national work, both because it blended these influences with the English poetic heritage of the past and because in the process it produced a characteristically English amalgam.

This was particularly noticeable in the way in which the influence of Castiglione's concept of the ideal courtier, which lay behind Spenser's professed intention in writing *The Faerie Queene*— 'to fashion a gentleman or noble person in virtuous and gentle discipline' underwent a thoroughly English acclimatization. For the heroes of *The Faerie Queene* are a mixture of medieval Christian knight and Elizabethan Puritan rather than typical 'men of the Renaissance'.

Not that Spenser himself did not respond, with all his senses, to the pagan worship of sensuous beauty. There is ample evidence in *The Faerie Queene* and in his other poems to prove that he did. But there was none of that gay and unquestioning surrender to it of which the Italians were capable: there was always a stern Puritan moral in reserve.

This ambivalence of attitude was itself, of course, typically English and one of the underlying characteristics of the whole period. It revealed itself particularly in relation to Italy which often stood at one and the same time for the heights of beauty and the depths of depravity. And although it sometimes resulted in hypocrisy, it also produced fruitful tensions, as John Milton, another great Puritan and lover of Italy, was likewise to prove.

It was not here that the weakness of *The Faerie Queene* lay. Neither was it in the allegorical framework, for the Elizabethan public was still close enough to the Middle Ages to appreciate it. Some of the most vivid parts of the poem—notably the cantos describing the Cave of Despair, and those dealing with the Seven Deadly Sins—are those closest to the medieval tradition. The weakness was rather that in his choice and handling of the medieval romances upon which he based the various episodes, especially the Arthurian stories, Spenser was attaching himself to a past that was already fading, and doing so in a nostalgic, almost escapist spirit, similar to that which we noted in the case of Malory's *Morte d'Arthure*.

Spenser was, therefore, to some extent outside the forces that were shaping the England of his day—partly no doubt because of his actual isolation for so much of his life in Ireland—and this remoteness is evident in the poetry of *The Faerie Queene* which, in spite of its descriptive and musical beauties, tends to be studied and over-literary. Perhaps that is why few people read the poem today, and why those who do have the sensation of wandering through a disused gallery hung with antique and heavily brocaded tapestries beautiful in detail but overwhelming in the mass.

Although, moreover, his fertility of invention (not only in the poems we have mentioned but in many others, such as the *Prothalamion* and the *Epithalamion*, to take two examples of outstanding beauty) earned him the title of 'the poets' poet', the value of his later influence is open to some doubt. It can often be seen, for example, that poets in their Spenserian phase (particularly when they are using the famous 'Spenserian stanza' of *The Faerie Queene*) are at their most contrived and precious. The Spenserian tradition, for all its long history, has not been the main line of English poetry. There was at least some justice in Ben Jonson's criticism of Spenser, that 'affecting the ancients, he writ no language'.

In spite of the undoubted greatness and originality of Spenser's genius it was a lesser poet, and one to whom Spenser dedicated *The Faerie Queene*, who more truly marked the dawn of the Renaissance of English poetry. Sir Philip Sidney, it is true, had a good deal in common with Spenser: he too was fascinated by the romances of chivalry, and in his work we find a similar blend of Platonism and Puritanism. His personal reputation as a chivalrous

Christian knight and a devout Protestant made him seem, indeed, like one of the heroes of *The Faerie Queene*—and in fact there is little doubt that Spenser had him in mind as one of his models.

But whereas Spenser was dependent on a patron whom he had to follow to Ireland for long years of exile, Sidney belonged to a great aristocratic family and was always at the centre of affairs. Suffering none of Spenser's frustrations, the past was for Sidney a matter of one lively interest among many rather than an emotional necessity. Politician, diplomat, soldier, courtier, and scholar he was the embodiment of the chivalrous ideal adapted to the need of the Renaissance—as described in Castiglione's book.

The sonnets, songs, and other lyrical pieces contained in *Sir P.S., His Astrophel and Stella* (published posthumously in 1591, a year after the appearance of Book I of *The Faerie Queene*) reveal most of the qualities of mature Elizabethan poetry. They are eloquent, passionate, and full of personal feeling, but at the same time they rely upon a set of recognized conventions and upon the formal rules of rhetoric and logic.

It was now, indeed, that the earlier books on rhetoric and prosody proved their value. With inferior poets they led to a good deal of bombast and hair-splitting, but they helped poets of Sidney's stature to combine lyricism and intellectual control. The 'conceits' of the Elizabethans and the mental acrobatics of the 'Metaphysical poets' of the seventeenth century, as well as the exercises in 'wit' of the eighteenth-century poets, all indirectly owed a good deal to this tradition of training in rhetoric and logic, and it could be argued that the emotional excesses of some of the poets of the Romantic Revival were in part due to its disappearance.

The vitality of the poetic outburst that followed showed itself in the astonishing variety of its forms and manifestations. Courtiers like Sir Walter Raleigh, Sir Edward Dyer, Sir Fulke Greville, and Edward de Vere, Earl of Oxford, for example, harassed by Court intrigues, foreign adventures, or the cares of State, yet proved themselves capable of producing occasional masterpieces. Books of prose suddenly opened like caskets to disclose unexpected gems of poetry. Pedestrian plays redeemed themselves by bursts of song, and great ones thrust out lyrics, almost as afterthoughts, like blossoms on the topmost branches of a tree. Between 1591 and 1597, under the impulse of Sidney's *Astrophel and Stella* and to a lesser extent of Spenser's *Amoretti*, some twenty sonnet sequences appeared one after the other, of which those of Henry Constable,

35

Thomas Lodge, Barnabe Barnes, Samuel Daniel, and Michael Drayton were perhaps the most distinguished.

Then there were the many pastorals, such as those of Nicholas Breton. The religious strain was exemplified by the poems of the Catholic Robert Southwell, who was to have a considerable influence upon seventeenth-century poets such as his co-religionist Richard Crashaw. A good deal of narrative poetry was also written—notably by Marlowe in *Hero and Leander*, and there were the two massive patriotic poems—the *Ciuill Warrs betweene the two houses of Lancaster and Yorke* by Samuel Daniel and the *Polyolbion* of Michael Drayton—described by an American critic as 'the megalosaurus and plesiosaurus of the Renaissance'. But in fairness to these two poets Daniel's beautiful and melodious dialogue of *Ulisses and the Syren*, and Drayton's enchanting fairy poem *Nymphidia* must also be mentioned. The satires of Joseph Hall, John Marsden, and John Donne initiated a tradition that was to reach its climax in the eighteenth century, and Sir John Davies's *Orchestra, or a Poem on Dancing*, with its curious play of fancy anticipated the Metaphysical poets.

And, of course, song was everywhere in Elizabethan England. It was to be found in town and country; on the stage and in the prose romances; in the market place, on the village green, and in the tavern. Songs appeared in the later collections such as *England's Helicon* and *England's Parnassus*, both published in 1600—and songs filled whole collections of their own, including the various *Bookes of Aires* by John Dowland and Thomas Campion.

Among the outstanding poems of the most prolific years of poetry-making in our history must be included George Chapman's translation (made between 1598 and 1609) of Homer's *Iliad*, which was to make such a powerful impression upon John Keats two hundred years later. It was one of a number of translations into poetry and prose in a period when England was belatedly but hungrily gathering to herself the fruits of humanism and the Renaissance.

For a time, however, it looked as if original English prose was in danger of strangling itself. There are a number of precedents to explain the disease of language known as 'Euphuism', as for instance the over-elaboration which was a characteristic of the prose of many of the Anglo-Saxon and medieval writers. The artifices of Malory, and the Latinized prose of earlier humanists such as Ascham, modelled on the antithetical style of Seneca, also played their part. There were, too, various foreign influences (notably that of the Spanish writer Guevara), and it has been

THE SECOND
PART OF THE
FAERIE QVEENE.

Containing

THE FOVRTH,
FIFTH, AND
SIXTH BOOKES.

By Ed. Spenſer.

Imprinted at London for VVilliam
Ponſonby. 1596.

Title-page to the second part of Spenser's *The Faerie Queene*, 1596

A page from Thomas Campion's *Book of Aires*, 1613

argued that the well-remembered rhythms of medieval plainsong contributed to the phenomenon.

The style of John Lyly's *Euphues, or the Anatomy of Wit* (1578)— from which the term euphuism derived—contained two distinct elements. There was, on the one hand, the principle of counter-poise and symmetry in sentences and clauses, together with an elaborate overlay of alliteration; and on the other there was the 'embellishment' of all kinds of images, metaphors, and illustrations drawn from mythology, ancient history, and particularly from the medieval and early Tudor herbaries, lapidaries and bestiaries. Between them these two devices created an effect of mathematical intricacy but also, to modern ears, of relentless monotony.

The prose of Sir Philip Sidney's *The Countesse of Pembroke's Arcadia* (1590)—a complicated romance full of pastoral and chivalrous adventures, which also contained songs—although it was not composed on quite as acrostic-like a pattern as *Euphues*, was every bit as elaborate. Between them indeed there is little doubt that Lyly and Sidney to some extent led English prose into a blind alley from which it did not fully emerge until the following century. But their influence was not entirely adverse. Euphuism performed a valuable service in bringing form to the formless and in setting positive standards of artistry, and both Lyly's and Sidney's stylistic experiments were largely the result of exuberance in an age when words for their own sake had an intoxicating effect.

Both *Euphues* and *Arcadia*, moreover, overgrown though their plots are by stylistic thickets, have a place in the evolution of English fiction. Sidney's romantic elaborations on human emotions and behaviour, in particular, marked a real advance in characterization and pointed forward to the sentimental refine-ments of Samuel Richardson, who indeed named one of his heroines, Pamela, after a character in *Arcadia*.

Fortunately, too, the stultifying effects of this kind of prose were to some extent offset by a powerful wave of realistic writing. In some of the best translations of the Italian *novelli*, for example, and in stories written under their influence, the vividness and freshness of the originals broke through, especially in those derived from Boccaccio. At the same time the popular tradition of story-telling maintained its vigour. The vogue of the Jest Books continued and the anecdotes they contained (the word 'Jest' or 'Geste', incidentally, meant 'act' or 'deed') were increasingly centred round a single character. It is indeed essential to remember that side by side with the literature of *Arcadia* ran this other literature of the market place and the tavern, the tradition upon which Shakespeare drew for his creation of Falstaff, and which also helped to lay the foundations of the English realistic novel. An important step in this same direction was the publication of Thomas Deloney's stories about the tradesmen and craftsmen of Elizabethan England, such as *The Pleasant Historie of John Winchcomb, in his younguer yeares called Jacke of Newbery*, which were close to the Jest Books in atmosphere and idiom—and which pointed forward to Daniel Defoe and eventually to Charles Dickens.

Equally important were the pamphlets about the Elizabethan underworld, such as Robert Greene's *A Notable Discoverie of Coosnage* (1591). The aim of these writers was ostensibly a moral one, but they threw themselves into depiction of low life with such gusto that one cannot help presuming not only a sneaking sympathy but a certain journalistic opportunism. Quite apart, too, from the fact that short stories were often embedded in these pamphlets they inaugurated a tradition of realistic *reportage* that culminated in the work of Daniel Defoe both in his pamphlets and historical writings and in his novels.

The high-water mark of fiction in this period, however, was Thomas Nashe's *The Unfortunate Traveller, Or the Life of Jacke Wilton* (1594) which is a genuine picaresque novel. Nashe's highly seasoned style, with its deceptively matter-of-fact tone in describing the horrors which his hero encounters has, moreover, a cumulative satirical effect which is comparable in many respects to that of Jonathan Swift in *A Modest Proposal*.

Nashe also devoted himself, with vigour, to the Martin Marprelate controversy—the most considerable of the pamphleteering battles of the period—which produced some of its most racy prose. It was brought about by an attempt of the Star Chamber in 1586 to check the flood of Puritan pamphlets—which provoked an unknown Puritan to counter with another series, inflaming passions, and pens, still further. But although Elizabethan prose was perhaps most at home in vituperation of this kind the period also produced, in Richard Hooker's *Of the Laws of Ecclesiastical Politie*, a model of clarity and dignity, while patriotism and the spirit of adventure found expression in the chronicles of Raphael Holinshed—one of the major influences in Shakespeare's History plays—and in *The Principall navigations, voiages and discoveries of the English made by sea or over land* of Richard Hakluyt (1589).

It was into the drama, however, that the English Renaissance poured its greatest imaginative energies. In comedy, the welter of conflicting traditions, conventions, influences, and tastes began to coalesce round about the year 1580. Thus the Court plays of John Lyly, a member of a group known as 'the University Wits', wove realistic farce, romantic fantasy, the allegory of the Morality Plays, the complexities of Latin comedy, mythological subjects, topical references and (not surprisingly) euphuistic wit into patterns more artistically complete than anything hitherto achieved in English comedy.

Similarly George Peel's *The Araygnement of Paris, a Pastorall*, which was played before the Court in 1580, illustrates that blend of court revels and folk-pastime which was one of the outstanding features of Elizabethan comedy. Two of Peele's other plays, *The Famous Chronicle of King Edward the first* and *The Old Wives' Tale* were still closer to folk-traditions, though the latter also contained elements of the Masque, and may have had some influence upon John Milton's *Comus*. In both *The Araygnement of Paris* and *The Old Wives' Tale* songs were included which were integral parts of the action.

Another important step forward (and by that phrase one usually means 'in the direction of Shakespeare') was accomplished by Robert Greene, one of the new class of professional writers who was poet, pamphleteer, and story-writer as well as playwright, when he brought together different types and classes of people, not merely as the passing figures in some Masque or Pageant but as part of an overall dramatic intention. Thus in *The Honorable Historie of Frier Bacon and Frier Bongay* (about 1589) magicians mingle with courtiers and kings, and a Prince of Wales woos Margaret the dairymaid of Fressingfield. What is more, the tale of magic and the tale of romantic love, though the narrative connexion between them is slight enough, nevertheless have a genuine symbolic correspondence, and constitute the first example in Elizabethan comedy of the use of parallel plot and sub-plot.

As far as tragedy was concerned it was Thomas Kyd who in his famous play *The Spanish Tragedie containing the lamentable end of Don Horatio and Bel-imperia: with the pitiful death of old Hieronimo* produced about 1590, gave the English theatre what at that juncture it needed. For Kyd took from Seneca what he knew the public enjoyed—the horrors and crimes and the revenge motif—without imitating his formal structure. At the same time he created in Hieronimo, seeking revenge for his murdered son, the most complete dramatic portrait to date, and though Kyd's language had plenty of Senecan bombast it also spoke in the authentic voice of tragedy.

The Spanish Tragedie initiated a whole series of 'revenge' plays. The greatest of them of course was Shakespeare's *Hamlet*, which owes something to Kyd's play, and other examples of the *genre* were Christopher Marlowe's *The Famous Tragedie of the Rich Jew of Malta*, John Marston's *Antonio's Revenge*, George Chapman's *The Revenge of Bussy d'Ambois*, and Cyril Tourneur's *The Revenger's Tragedie*. But it was the 'mighty line' of Christopher Marlowe (as Ben Jonson called it) which for the first time brought great poetry on to the English stage and which was to echo, like the sound of drums and trumpets, throughout the whole period.

Marlowe was in fact the first English playwright of real genius, possessed of a force and depth of imagination superior to anything that had gone before. The hero of his *Tamburlaine the Great* (the two parts were presented in 1587 and 1588) with his faith in the ecstasies of earthly glory, including those of love and power, and his readiness to challenge God and Death in their accomplishment marks a high point in the Renaissance glorification of man and coincided with a peak of national enthusiasm for real-life heroes such as Sir Francis Drake.

At the same time its horrors, its rhetoric, its moments of macabre comedy and above all the thunder of its verse made it a favourite with the 'groundlings'. One of Marlowe's great services to the English Theatre in fact was to produce a type of drama in which popular tastes and traditions finally joined forces with those of the Renaissance. Thus *The Tragical History of the Life and Death of Dr Faustus* (1588), the first great tragedy of humanism, was derived from a popular pamphlet (and there was a ballad on the same subject): the farcical elements are clearly reminiscent of those in some Miracle Plays and in the most popular of the Interludes as well as of the horse-play in the popular Jigs. The play is also a Morality in the sense that it is a struggle between Good and Evil. But at the same time the central character is no abstract quality, but a real man who dares and sins and suffers—as magnificent in his own kind of tragic defiance as Tamburlaine himself. And though *The troublesome Raigne and lamentable Death of Edward II King of England* lacked the dramatic fire of the two great tragedies it was a great advance on the earlier formless chronicle plays and demonstrated a new subtlety and maturity of characterization.

In considering the drama of the English Renaissance we must

remember that between 1580 and 1642, when the Puritans closed
the public theatres, performances were taking place simultaneously
in the London theatres of all kinds of plays, not to mention those
presented in private houses and in the provinces. A large proportion
of the tremendous output needed to meet all these demands has
been lost, and of that which has survived we have only glanced at
a tiny part. We have done so, too, as if the whole of Elizabethan
drama was centred round Shakespeare. So it is as far as we are
concerned, but in his own time he was only one of a number of
playwrights, many of whom pursued strongly independent lines
and had important contributions to make. To take the most outstanding example Ben Jonson (whom many of his contemporaries
regarded as Shakespeare's superior) produced an entirely new
type of realistic comedy combining the approach of the old
Moralities with the conventions of Latin comedy, as well as
writing tragedies constructed on classical lines.

What is certain, though, is that all the forces, popular and
learned, medieval and contemporary, national and foreign that
went to the making of the English Renaissance fused in Shakespeare to produce its most brilliant phenomenon and one that
belongs, moreover, to world literature.

To begin with the poetry: we can see classical learning blending
with Italian influences in *Venus and Adonis* and *The Rape of
Lucrece* to produce the only considerable examples apart from
Marlowe's *Hero and Leander* of Italianate erotic poetry—and at the
same time already giving evidence of qualities of characterization
and dramatic insight. The *Sonnets*, some of which were probably
written as early as 1588, contain a depth and range of experience
that transformed a convention which in other hands was seldom
entirely free from literary artifice.

The song, too, Shakespeare used with a new subtlety of ironic
or dramatic effect to point the action or to mark changes of mood
and atmosphere, both in comedies such as *Twelfth Night, or What
You Will* and *A Winter's Tale* and in tragedies such as *Othello*.

Above all of course there is the blank verse which in Shakespeare's hands reached its highest peaks of development. Influenced
by Marlowe's 'mighty line' in the earlier History plays, it rapidly
became an instrument of astonishing flexibility, able to render
the smallest nuances of thought, feeling, and characterization, so
that even the most minor characters have their own individual,
immediately recognizable idiom. In the great tragedies it triumphantly encompassed the most profound probings into the nature

of man's destiny that literature has ever attempted, and in the later plays it took on yet further qualities of music and symbolism. It was a process of continuous development and adaptation in response both to the changing needs of the theatre and to the demands of Shakespeare's personal experience.

The quality of Shakespeare's response to language was indeed apparent from the very beginning. In *Love's Labour's Lost* (1591), for example, he was as intoxicated by words as any of his contemporaries but already he was displaying a sharper ear and a deeper awareness. The brilliant 'sets of wit' themselves had dramatic relevance and one of Shakespeare's great themes, that of the contrast between real love and self-deception in love, was already present. So too was the beginning of the Shakespearean comic tradition, while the play as a whole was a more satisfying dramatic whole than any of the courtly comedies of Lyly which it set out to rival.

The linguistic preoccupation continued for some time, but with each new play there was also an impressive advance towards dramatic maturity. Thus much of the language of *Romeo and Juliet* (1594) is still artificial and literary—but it can also render magnificently the bravado and tragedy of youth while in the Nurse—who uses quite another kind of language to remind us of the earthy, physical side of romantic love—we have the first of Shakespeare's really great comic creations. In *The Merchant of Venice* (1594) linguistic indulgences disappear the moment the action demands a more serious utterance, and in *Much Ado About Nothing* (1597) the 'sets of wit' between Benedick and Beatrice are perfectly related to character.

As early as 1594 *A Midsummer Night's Dream*, with its four worlds of the court, the lovers, the fairies, and the 'rude mechanicks', with its amazing dexterity of plot and its blend of fancy, realism, and sophisticated entertainment, was making the experiments of Lyly, Peele, and Greene in the same direction look clumsy and amateurish. And by the time he wrote *Twelfth Night* (1601) Shakespeare did not even need to separate out his various social levels into different plots, for they are all naturally brought together in a single one—and in this play we are in the presence of a virtuosity so perfect that romance, realism, revelry, comedy, poetry, prose, music, and song are all completely integrated leaving no unresolved residue of any kind behind.

The same power of transcending existing traditions and fashions showed itself in Shakespeare's history plays. The first of them leaned heavily upon the chronicles and contemporary plays based upon them, as well as upon Kyd and Marlowe as far as style was concerned, but *Richard III* (1591) was already suggesting a new and potentially tragic concept of character in relation to public events, while in *King John* (1594) we see the old rambling chronicle play transformed into a powerful dramatic unity. The two parts of *Henry IV* (1597) with *Henry V* (1597) as a kind of epilogue, with their profound insight into the realities of political responsibility and power, carry the tradition to its highest point of development.

The character of Falstaff in *Henry IV* provides yet another example of the transforming, universalizing power of Shakespeare's genius. In his bare bones (if one dare apply such a term to Falstaff) he is a combination of the abstract characters such as Gluttony, Sloth, and Lechery of the medieval Seven Deadly Sins and of the Morality Plays, and of the 'boastful soldier' of Latin comedy. In Shakespeare's hands he becomes not only a link between the worlds of the court and the tavern, an ironic commentator upon the theme of 'honour', a perpetual reminder that there is another side to the coin, but also a comic poem or epic in his own right—a separate play almost, but one that sets its comic and funda-mentally human vitality against the false and feverish vitality of political ambition and power.

Then again we can see how humanism came to its full flowering in Shakespeare. Its classical aspect was represented in the Roman plays starting with *Julius Caesar* (1597) which, like the English histories was concerned with political realism but which in the character of Brutus created a new and psychologically more subtle reaction to it—and culminating with *Antony and Cleopatra* (1606) where the worlds of politics and love are brought into tragic conflict. The Renaissance aspect of humanism, on the other hand, found its profoundest representative in Hamlet, the student of Wittenberg.

In addition *Hamlet, Prince of Denmark* (1601) bears witness—as in the case of the plays of the final phase—to the quickness of Shake-speare's response to changing tastes in the theatre. For the production coincided with a renewed vogue for the Senecan drama of blood and revenge. But again Shakespeare's touch transforms everything for the revenge motif is infinitely deepened by the complication of the hero's conscience and whatever other motives might lie behind his procrastination. One has only to consider contemporary tragedies in the same *genre*—which were in fact beginning to reveal symptoms of the decline of the great

Elizabethan dramatic impetus—to realize the magnitude of Shakespeare's achievement. Far from showing a decline *Hamlet* exhibits fresh resources of vitality and invention: to take only one example—the soliloquy, which in the past had been mainly a vehicle for conveying information, in *Hamlet* became a new and powerful medium for the *dramatic* revelation of character and motive.

Hamlet is related too to the 'problem' or 'bitter' comedies, such as *Measure for Measure* (1601) which, partly in response to the morbidity of the age and partly no doubt in response to the actualities of Shakespeare's own experience, savagely call in question the validity of love, honour, mercy, and justice. It belongs too, of course, to the great tragedies, in which this questioning is pushed to its furthest extremes; in which all the positive values of life are turned upside-down and scrutinized with merciless objectivity—so that in *Macbeth* (1606) 'fair is foul, and foul is fair' and in *King Lear* (1606) the order of Nature itself seems to be reversed—and from which a new and redemptive vision is snatched out of the furnace of intolerable suffering.

Mr. WILLIAM

SHAKESPEARES

COMEDIES,
HISTORIES, &
TRAGEDIES.

Publiſhed according to the True Originall Copies.

Martin Droeshout ſculpſit London

LONDON
Printed by Iſaac Iaggard, and Ed. Blount. 1623.

Title-page to the First Folio Shakespeare

testum

porticus

sedilia

orchestra

mimorum ædes.

ingressus

proscænium.

planities siue arena.

Ex obseruationibus Londinensibus
Johannis de witt

Interior of the Old Swan Theatre, Bankside

3 · An Age of Transition

THE division of literature into centuries and periods is merely an artificial convenience for historians. In reality past, present, and future merge into each other by imperceptible degrees.

It would, for example, be wrong to assume that the kind of literature described by the word 'Elizabethan' suddenly came to an end with the death of Queen Elizabeth. Indeed the Queen was already an old woman before the great cultural flowering associated with her name really began, and yet during her lifetime symptoms of a new age were already making themselves felt. Similarly during the reign of James I there were many manifestations of the 'Elizabethan' spirit, just as there were many that looked forward to the future.

Sir Walter Raleigh, for example, whose career and personality seem almost to symbolize the age of 'Gloriana' and who has been described as 'the last of the Elizabethans', revealed in his later work an intensity of poetic argumentation combined with personal melancholy that relate him to the 'Metaphysical poets' as much as to the Elizabethans. John Donne, the chief of the 'Metaphysical poets' wrote his *Satires* and most of the *Elegies* as well as the *Songs and Sonets* in the 1590s, and Ben Jonson, in many ways the most representative figure of a new age, also wrote much of his poetry during the reign of Elizabeth.

On the other hand Michael Drayton (who lived until 1631) was a typical Elizabethan to the end, and William Drummond of Hawthornden, who did not publish his first volume of poems until 1616, wrote typically Elizabethan love sonnets and madrigals. Typically Elizabethan songs, too, crop up frequently in the plays and masques of the seventeenth century, and Thomas Campion's fourth *Book of Aires* was published in 1613.

There were similar overlaps in prose. Richard Hooker's *Of the Laws of Ecclesiastical Politie* (1593), although typical of the Elizabethan age in many ways, also looked forward to the more cogent and controlled use of prose associated with the seventeenth and eighteenth centuries. On the other hand Jeremy Taylor, author of *Holy Living* (1650) and *Holy Dying* (1651) has been described as 'the Shakespeare and Spenser of the pulpit'.

'Elizabethan' drama, moreover, did not reach its climax until the seventeenth century. Shakespeare's great tragic period began with the production of *Hamlet* in 1602, continued through the great Roman tragedies and the plays of 'the final phase' culminating in *The Tempest* (1609–11).

All the same, it is only necessary to reflect upon these plays to be struck by the contrast the underlying mood and temper afford with the earlier buoyant Shakespeare, a contrast that cannot be explained on the grounds of personal and creative history alone. Shakespeare's later plays, in fact, *do* suggest that a profound change in the climate of English thought and feeling—and therefore in the literature it nourished—more or less coincided with the end of the sixteenth and the beginning of the seventeenth centuries.

The fundamental reason for this change was the growing realization that humanism, instead of being an invincible guarantee of man's progress and stability, as it had appeared in its glorious heyday, was itself shot through with uncertainties and contradictions.

The religious traditions of the Middle Ages were still powerful and these came increasingly into conflict with the secular values of the Renaissance. Many people, while believing that it was right that the individual should be freed from the rigid Scholastic system that had robbed him of his potency, were nevertheless concerned as to what might be sacrificed in the process. What effect, for example, would the doctrine of individualism have upon the 'social order'? Anxiety on this score deepened as the sixteenth century progressed. For example, while the stress on the necessity for strong central government in Shakespeare's early history plays is in the main related to the success of the Tudor monarchy in bringing to an end the chaos of civil conflict, in the later plays, such as *Troilus and Cressida* with its famous speech by Ulysses on 'degree', the principle of 'order' in human and social affairs and in Nature, is subjected to a far more searching analysis, and the awareness of the chaos underlying human aspirations takes on a tragic profundity. A similar concern runs through Hooker's *Ecclesiastical Politie* and it may be said to have reached its climax in the grim vision of human society, growing out of actual experience of civil war, in *The Leviathan* of Thomas Hobbes (1651), while after the Restoration the overriding demand in social and cultural life as well as in politics was for order and balance.

This conflict between the religious traditions of the Middle Ages and the secular values of the Renaissance was no doubt brought to a head by economic causes. At the height of their power, the Tudor aristocrats had more or less succeeded in being both great country magnates—bringing protection and economic security to their dependents—and great courtiers. But as time went by they were undermined by rising costs and by the growing rise of capitalism. Absentee landlordism became more and more common and the last years of Elizabeth's reign witnessed a constant squandering of estates together with a scramble for wealth and privilege at court—particularly for the new commercial monopolies—and an ever-increasing ostentation and display. In the reign of James I these symptoms became even more acute, and it is significant that it was in this period, when self-interest and personal greed were at their most barefaced, that the cynical principles of Machiavelli received particularly wide currency. It is in fact Machiavelli who represents the dark reverse side of the coin of Renaissance individualism.

These factors (among many others) combined with the atmosphere of political and religious intrigue that attended the last years of Elizabeth and the sordid aspects of James I's court and personality, the threatening shadow of Puritanism, and perhaps the first premonitions of the Civil War, to produce a mood of melancholy and disillusionment in which life seemed lacking in constructive purpose, human nature to be ugly and perverse, and society to be vitiated and corrupt. In addition there was the impact of the 'new philosophy' of Copernicus which (though at first regarded merely as one theory among many others) threatened further to undermine traditional ways of thinking and further emphasized man's moral isolation.

It was a mood which inevitably led to an increase in scepticism, introspection, self-consciousness, and self-criticism, and therefore a growing emphasis in literature upon realism and satire, a more inward sense of tragedy, a more subjective response to experience, and a deeper analysis of behaviour and motive. In thought, moreover, it led to a gradual separation of faith and reason and to the beginnings of empirical science, so that by the time of the Restoration of 1660 English culture presented a very different picture. The seventeenth century, in fact, was an age of transition in which the Middle Ages, the Renaissance, and the modern world met for the first time.

It was in the field of the drama that English humanism had achieved its greatest imaginative triumphs, and it was here that

47

its decline made itself most apparent. For one thing there were important changes in the theatre and its relationship to the public. At one time humanism had been the great unifying force in the drama, and its most ardent representatives had also been those who commanded most popular support. But as the Puritans became increasingly powerful the actors were forced to depend more and more upon the court, and the complexion of their audiences gradually changed. In 1609, for example, Shakespeare's company began to concentrate on their 'private' theatre at Blackfriars which was too expensive for the 'groundlings'—and before long it became more important than the popular Globe Theatre. This instance is symptomatic of a separation between the courtly and fashionable sections of the theatre-going public on the one hand, and ordinary folk on the other—a separation which rapidly widened as time went by.

Drama in consequence began to lose its contact with the folk-traditions that had constituted one of its main strengths. Although playwrights like Thomas Dekker and Thomas Heywood were still writing for the popular stage as late as 1630, others such as Francis Beaumont and John Fletcher tended to concentrate upon the narrower task of catering for a fashionable *élite*.

One of the outstanding examples of the growing gap between the two kinds of public was the emergence of the Masque. This was a form of entertainment which combined song, music, dancing, recitative, and dialogue (and can therefore be regarded as one of the ancestors of opera) and which was presented with the aid of elaborate stagecraft and scenery. These masques often contained fine poetry and as Inigo Jones, the great architect, designed many of them and the music was frequently written by the best composers of the day they were often of great aesthetic beauty. But like the earlier Interludes they were mostly confined to the Court and to private houses.

Under these circumstances it was not surprising that symptoms of a decline in the great tradition of the drama began to show themselves. The usual exception has to be made in the case of Shakespeare. It is one of the signs of his supreme genius that he could adapt himself to changing conditions and utilize them for yet further explorations into the mysteries of human existence. His understanding of the tragic implications inherent in the contradictions and weaknesses of humanism was, in any case, more profound than that of his contemporaries. The growing disillusionment of the age had already been reflected in his later sonnets and in the 'bitter comedies', and it reached its highest expression in the disgust and self-disgust of *Hamlet*—and above all in the terrible vision of a world handed over to violence and brute instinct that is *King Lear*. Some of the speeches of Edmund in this play can in fact be seen as the most damning indictment of individualism, divorced, after the manner of Machiavelli, from all moral sanctions. Only Hobbes's vision of the life of man outside society as 'poor, nasty, brutish, and short' was to come anywhere near it in intensity.

Most of the other tragedians of the period reflected the prevailing mood without, on the whole, rising above it. Their plays were rather tainted by it, so that they themselves contained the elements of disintegration. Many of these playwrights seem to have been under a compulsion to present human nature in its worst light. They usually turned for their plots to the darkest side of Renaissance Italy—the world of sinister political intrigue and corruption associated with the Borgias—and went out of their way to emphasize its crimes, perversions, and treacheries.

John Webster's two tragedies *The White Devil* and *The Duchess of Malfi* are characteristic. They are saved from mere melodrama because Webster's conception of life as pitiless and corrupt has a certain poetic intensity and contains flashes of lyrical feeling and compassion. On the other hand his vision is not sufficiently powerful—as was that of Shakespeare in *King Lear*—to provide a real unifying principle or to envisage the possibilities of renewal and redemption. There is in consequence an incompleteness and scrappiness in his plays which reflect the prevailing moral and philosophical uncertainty. The best scenes tend to be theatrical in the pejorative sense and in characterization the stress is too often on the highly coloured and the grotesque. The people of his plays are like rapid thumb-nail sketches and do not bear that organic relationship with each other or with a common background that distinguishes the great period of 'Elizabethan' tragedy. They are brilliant but splintered refractions of the Elizabethan imaginative vision and in consequence Webster's plays seem to be constructed of innumerable ingeniously mortised fragments, rather than carved out of the solid block.

The world of Cyril Tourneur is even more corrupt than that of Webster; his characters are more like the Vices of the old Morality Plays than human beings; the combination of grotesque satire and moral allegory is, however, typical of some of the best work in tragedy during this period. The most 'Shakespearian' of the

49

seventeenth-century Italianate tragedies are perhaps Thomas Middleton's *Women Beware Women* and *The Changeling* for they were plays conceived in human and realistic rather than melodramatic terms.

Writers of tragedy such as Beaumont and Fletcher, however, became more and more concerned with the search for startling plots and effects, and the world they portrayed became increasingly unreal and extravagant. They revealed remarkable stagecraft; their plots were compact and their dramatic effects dexterous; the scenic and theatrical qualities were of a high order and the versification often easy and fluent. But fundamentally their works are contrived; the emotions are forced and artificial and expressed in high-flown set speeches. As with many modern films the response they invite is that of a 'good cry' rather than that 'purging of the emotions' which Aristotle had laid down as the purpose of true tragedy.

Beaumont and Fletcher were in fact, first and foremost entertainers, and their growing attachment to sentimental tragicomedy demonstrates how little real concern they had for the tragic vision of life. Their main preoccupation was to cater for a new fashionable public which demanded a momentary titivation of the emotions rather than a profound dramatic experience. With Thomas Heywood, sentiment and introspective morality take the place of real tragic intensity and suggest the emergence of the kind of middle-class tastes that were to find their natural outlet in the novel.

John Ford is often a graceful poet, not without psychological subtlety, but his only real subject, the pathos of suffering, is a poor substitute for the comprehensive tragic vision of the great Elizabethan playwrights. His handling of it, moreover, is vitiated by a kind of morbid inquisitiveness accompanied by an equally morbid interest in the refinements of cruelty and perversity.

But there still remains one other dramatist of great and independent genius whose tragedies certainly displayed none of the symptoms of decadence, but whose case needs to be taken separately.

Ben Jonson was one of the most learned of the English Humanists and his two Roman tragedies are full of quotations from Latin authors including the inevitable Seneca. They also have the scope and dignity of authentic tragedy. But though in quality they are part of the Elizabethan tradition they stand somewhat apart from the mainstream. Jonson was a reformer of the drama who—

like Sir Philip Sidney—scoffed at the loosely constructed type of play, which was nevertheless the Elizabethan norm. The tragic world revealed in his plays, for all its impressiveness, has nothing like the variety and richness of Shakespeare's. It does not absorb the reader emotionally and imaginatively—on the contrary it calls for quite a different sort of participation. For Jonson was fundamentally a moralist and a satirist of the later stages of humanism. Often his aim was to expose his hero's arrogant and impious craving for power. To 'expose' rather than to 'reveal'—and the distinction between the two words underlines the difference in intention between Jonson and most of the Elizabethan dramatists and between the societies to which they belonged. Where Marlowe had been able to invest the 'will to power' with a certain glamour, as a manifestation of the Renaissance spirit at its most daring and confident—by the time of Jonson it was becoming only too evident that it was exactly this elevation of the human will that constituted its greatest moral weakness. Jonson could no longer be dazzled by an individualism that increasingly manifested itself in a cynical and amoral 'realism' and he set out to demonstrate that its glitter was fundamentally spurious and evil.

Ben Jonson was not indeed the only playwright of the period to use tragedy for satirical purposes, but it was he more than any who analysed the effects of the crisis in humanism upon the social behaviour of his day. This was even more evident in his comedies, which certainly contain much boisterous and amusing farce, but which are not far removed from the spirit of tragedy in their indictment of a world dominated by greed and lust.

Jonson's theory of 'humours', exemplified in *Everyman in his Humour* and *Everyman out of his Humour* obviously bears a close resemblance to the methods of the old Morality Plays. But they are also related to the 'Character' writers of the seventeenth century—and look forward to the caricature approach of some of the novelists. The bustling raucous world of his comedies, with its crowds of rich and colourful personalities has, indeed, much in common with that of Dickens.

It is only necessary, moreover, to place the setting of Jonson's *Bartholomew Fair*—to choose an example which according to some critics is particularly 'Dickensian'—beside Shakespeare's Forest of Arden to see how great is the contrast between Shakespearian and Jonsonian comedy. Jonson's approach was basically realistic and contemporary while that of Shakespeare—though of course he too was a realist in another sense—was romantic and timeless. This kind of realism, almost documentary in its detail, relates Jonson not only to the 'comedy of manners' of the Restoration, but also to the prose and verse satirists of the eighteenth century—as well as to Hogarth whose paintings of his own contemporary scene are typically 'Jonsonian' in manner and approach.

The other comedies of the seventeenth century (apart of course from those of Shakespeare) are of minor importance by comparison. Philip Massinger's *A New Way to Pay Old Debts*, a bitter satire of the rising commercial classes, and many of Middleton's farcical comedies too are close to Jonson in realism and satirical intention. On the other hand Thomas Dekker's *The Shoemaker's Holiday*, though it has some affinities to Jonson, retains much of the sunny quality of Elizabethan romantic comedy and at the same time contains a vein of sentimentality likely to appeal to the rising middle classes. Others of his plays have elements, especially in the characterization, which look forward to the novels of Samuel Richardson. Beaumont and Fletcher's *The Knight of the Burning Pestle* also deals with the world of London tradesmen and apprentices but, though its burlesque of middle-class tastes and sentiments is remarkably adroit, it lacks Dekker's humanity and warmth. Its prime aim is again surface entertainment rather than insight into character and situation.

To sum up, therefore, as far as drama is concerned—although both tragedies and comedies continued to be written in considerable numbers right up to the closing of the theatres in 1642, the great tradition was slowly dying and would have come to an end even without the intervention of the Puritans. Whereas in the Elizabethan period the drama had attracted the best and most poetic minds, in the seventeenth century it is in other literary forms that they must increasingly be sought, particularly in the field of non-dramatic poetry.

It has already been pointed out that much of seventeenth-century poetry had its roots in the Elizabethan world. Ben Jonson's three collections for example were Elizabethan in many respects, especially in the lyrics. But his short satirical pieces, his moral satires, and his epistles (with their debts to Horace), his elegies and epitaphs (inspired by the Greek Anthology) mark him out as a classicist above all else. His commendatory verses—such as the famous lines addressed to Shakespeare—and his Pindaric

Design by Inigo Jones for the House of Fame in *The Masque of Queenes* by
Ben Jonson, performed 2 February 1609

II.

Oh that my wayes were directed to keepe thy Statutes. Ps. 119. 5.

w. Simpson Sculp:

Engraving by Simpson from Francis Quarles's *Emblemes*, London 1635

odes contain elements for example, that link him to John Dryden.

Of Ben Jonson's followers one of the most notable was Robert Herrick, a miniaturist whose lyrics breathe of the English countryside with its fairs and festivals, its dances and its folk-lore—though his language has a polish and neatness that again anticipates the Augustans.

It is however the 'Metaphysical poets' who seem to us now to be most characteristic of the period. The phrase was first applied to them by Dr Johnson, to denote the complicated nature of their mental and emotional processes and the kind of imagery they used to express them.

Dr Johnson, writing in an age where balance, order, neatness, and precision were the poetic ideals, disapproved of many of these features, though, as so often happens in his criticism, in analysing the reasons for his opinions he strikes time after time at the heart of the matter. Thus his phrase 'the most heterogeneous ideas yoked by violence together' really does describe the basic method of these poets—and the implied criticism is justified when it misfires. But at its best the method was an effective way of bringing together an astonishing range of interests, and when it was employed with passion, as in John Donne, even the 'violence' justified itself. As Johnson himself had to admit: 'if their conceits were far-fetched they were often worth the carriage'.

Metaphysical poetry was not as unrelated a phenomenon as has been sometimes assumed and some of its earlier antecedents have already been mentioned. But what was new was a heightening of nervous sensibility connected with the underlying tensions of the period, that enabled the best of the 'Metaphysical poets' to fuse the experiences of the intellect and of the emotions into imaginatively powerful combinations, so that—as T. S. Eliot has said—'the intellect was immediately at the tips of the senses'.

A striking example of this fusion, so complete that it is impossible to say where thought ends and feeling begins—and the thought *is* feeling and the feeling thought—is provided by two lines from John Donne's *The Progresse of the Soule*:

> '. . . her pure, and eloquent blood
> Spoke in her cheeks, and so distinctly wrought
> That one might almost say, her body thought.'

Although Donne drew his conceits from a wide range of learning many of them derive from homely and everyday

53

experience and the overall effect of his poetry is usually the reverse of pedantic. On the contrary it is the sense of vivid, living speech that most strikes the reader.

It is *personal*, not public utterance, moreover. Sir Thomas Wyatt had to some extent forestalled him in this respect, but for the most part Elizabethan poetry had been controlled by the rules of Rhetoric. As recent scholars have pointed out Donne's methods too probably conform to these rules, but his practice undoubtedly marks a new departure, particularly the way in which he used the short lyric or song to explore and analyse his experience of love in an infinite variety of moods. His famous poem *The Sunne Rising* with its colloquial opening: 'Busie old foole, unruly Sunne . . .' is a good example of a method which forces the reader into active participation, so that he has the feeling that stress, intonation, and gesture are created as he reads—as if the poet himself were arguing, pleading, or expostulating in his presence. At the same time the rhythmic effect is never confined to the single line, but envelops the whole stanza, while the separate stanzas combine to create a total effect, almost as if they were the acts of a well-made play.

In his *Satires* and *Elegies* too, Donne's method, as he twists and bends the couplet to make it serve all the subtle variations and emphases of intimate colloquial speech, is essentially dramatic. It is only in the great playwrights that a comparable range and urgency of expression can be found. There is no basic change of style or approach in Donne's religious poetry. He explores his experiences with the same passionate intensity and with the same startling imagery, sometimes learned, sometimes homely, and he addresses God with the same variety of tone and mood as he had his mistresses. A notable consequence was that the *Holy Sonnets* gave the sonnet convention an entirely new dimension.

The learning upon which Donne drew was fundamentally Elizabethan and medieval—but his poetry also contains many references to 'the new philosophy' and the new scientific theories. In his response to them he displayed the melancholy characteristic of a period which demands profound reorientations of outlook and seems to threaten old ways of thought and feeling. In Donne and some of the other 'Metaphysical poets' this pessimism was expressed chiefly in theological terms—for instance in the idea that the contemporary *malaise* was symptomatic of a further stage in the fall of man, and that the end of the world was rapidly drawing near. But it is the underlying attitude that partly explains why in the 1920s—also a period of scientific revolution that made great demands upon men's powers of adjustment—the Metaphysical poets appeared to have a special relevance. Both T. S. Eliot and Ezra Pound, for example, made use of widely scattered elements of learning, in a manner that recalled Donne, to emphasize the cultural disintegration which, it seemed to them, was characteristic of the world in which they lived.

There is a considerable contrast between Donne's relationship with God and that of George Herbert—perhaps the next greatest of the 'Metaphysicals'. Donne's is stormy and passionate, a continual struggle to achieve union with God; Herbert's also involves conflict, but on the whole it is conflict 'recollected in tranquillity'. It is the record of a man who experiences the normal moments of doubt or even of serious revolt, but who is basically secure in his faith, and whose estrangements from God will inevitably be followed by reconciliation. With Donne it is faith in the process of 'becoming'; with Herbert it is faith in the state of 'being'. Donne's religious feeling is more powerful and intense, but Herbert's is more mature, and he represents the temper of the Anglican Church at its finest and most humane.

Herbert really belongs to the mainstream of religious poetry and is only incidentally one of the 'Metaphysicals'. But like them he makes use of unusual images and conceits, and some of these also reflect contemporary currents of thought, including the new interest in science. On the whole, however, he prefers conceits derived from domestic life, which give his poetry great freshness and charm, dispensing an aroma like that of sheets in lavender. His poetry, too, is more musical in the Elizabethan sense than Donne's, but his courtly urbanity links him as well with the Cavalier poets, and the neatness and point of his language with Ben Jonson—and ultimately with the poets of the eighteenth century.

Henry Vaughan's secular poetry was influenced by Ben Jonson, but, though he uses Metaphysical paradoxes, his poetry does not possess the intellectual toughness and precision of the best of the 'Metaphysicals'. It does, however, contain brilliant moments of religious illumination and flashes of intuitive communion with nature that anticipate some of the Romantics, especially Blake and Wordsworth.

Religion plays a smaller part in the poetry of Andrew Marvell, though he was an ardent Puritan and at one stage a tutor in the household of Oliver Cromwell. His work and personality reveal a blend of humanism in its more joyous aspects and of the kind of courtly urbanity not usually associated with the Puritans. In many respects Marvell reflects the finest and most humane elements among that part of the aristocracy, Puritan or Anglican, which threw in its lot with the Parliamentary cause in the Civil War.

Some of Marvell's most beautiful poems were inspired by a countryside setting but, though they contain a good deal of detailed personal observation of flowers, trees, and bird-song and an undoubted love of Nature, it is Nature in its civilized aspects that most appeals to Marvell. His real affection is for man-made gardens and orchards and landscape—an attitude that has more in common with that of Augustan poets. But the imagery supplied by this background is typically 'Metaphysical' in its wit and ingenuity, as in *Upon Appleton House*, where the ranks of flowers are brought into subtle and moving relation with the soldiers of the Civil War.

It is, however, in Marvell's religious and philosophical poems that the true Metaphysical strain is most marked as it is also in his great love poem *To his Coy Mistress*.

Abraham Cowley employed language and imagery in ways typical of the school, but without the unifying imagination of the best of them. His rational temper and his interest in the new scientific spirit manifested themselves in some of his *Odes*, and both the subject-matter and the form of these relate him closely with the Augustans—particularly John Dryden whose early work he probably influenced.

One other group of poets contribute an important strand to the pattern of seventeenth-century poetry, though, at first sight, they seem to stand apart from it. These were the 'Cavalier poets' of the reign of Charles I who restored to court poetry—which in the previous reign had tended towards exaggerated sentiment and heroic bombast—something of the dignity and order of the Elizabethan tradition.

There is, however, one great difference between the verses of the Cavalier poets and those of the Elizabethans: though they were fluent and melodious they were less directly dependent upon music for their associations and effects. They are closer to cultivated speech than to song, and their imagery is often more intellectual than that of the typical Elizabethan lyric. The method of such poets as Richard Lovelace is, in spite of the lightness of tone, a dialectical one, and Cavalier poetry was by no means un-affected by that of the 'Metaphysicals'. Thus Sir John Suckling's poems in their colloquial ease and informality, and in their cynical attitude, have a good deal in common with the lighter love poems of John Donne.

The aristocratic grace and frequent licentiousness of these poets was in marked contrast to the moral didacticism of the Puritans, but in fact they were not without serious qualities as Thomas Carew—perhaps the most considerable among them—demon-strated in his fine elegy on John Donne. The lyrics of the Restoration court poets were crude by comparison and in their classical neatness of expression the Cavalier poets look beyond them to the Augustans.

The outstanding poetic achievement of the age, however, was that of John Milton, and it is he who most completely embodies its cultural and religious traditions as well as its innermost con-flicts and aspirations. Yet, paradoxically, it is difficult to think of him in terms of the processes shaping English literature, or to associate him with any category other than that which he occupies in magnificent and awe-inspiring isolation.

It is not that his literary relationships are obscure: he himself sang the praises of his mentors from Chaucer onwards, declaring that Spenser was his master, rendering homage to Shakespeare in some of his most impressive verses, and expressing his approval of Ben Jonson's 'learned sock'. Elizabethan characteristics are apparent not only in some of his youthful poems, in his first masterpiece the *Ode on the Morning of Christ's Nativity* (1629), and in the famous 'mood' poems *L'Allegro* and *Il Penseroso* composed in 1638—but also in the lyrical passages of *Paradise Lost* and par-ticularly in the lovely description in Book II of Adam and Eve in the Garden of Eden. The influence of Elizabethan pastoral, too, is evident in the great elegy *Lycidas*. In the earlier poems, more-over, the classical learning and the underlying seriousness of purpose were lightened by the presence of those vigorous folk-elements that nourished some of the best of Elizabethan poetry, and it must also be remembered that like Chaucer he travelled in Italy and opened himself to the sunshine of the Renaissance.

To some extent, too, he responded to the fashions of the seven-teenth century. Thus *Comus* was a Masque presented at Ludlow Castle, with music composed by Henry Lawes—though the strong moral intention behind its characters also related it to the Morality Plays. He also tried his hand on occasion at the 'Metaphysical' manner, as in the early poem *The Passion* and even in certain passages of *Paradise Lost* itself.

But there are elements in Milton's work and personality that make such considerations largely irrelevant. First and foremost there was the dedication from an early age to the task of becoming a great poet, which meant that in Milton there was little of the unconscious absorption of literary influences that attends most poets. In a man of lesser genius this might have led to over-conscious contrivance, but in Milton the deliberation of purpose was backed not only by massive learning but also by impressive powers of intellect and imagination. Admittedly Spenser, too, had also dedicated himself with equal seriousness to the task of becoming a great national Protestant poet. But where as in *The Faerie Queene*, Spenser had succeeded only spasmodically in blending the spirit of the Renaissance and that of the Reformation, producing tracts of moral discourse illuminated by passages of sensuous beauty, Milton triumphantly achieved the synthesis, so that in the work of his maturity the art and the religious purpose became one.

This synthesis had indeed already been foreshadowed earlier but it is, of course, *Paradise Lost* that marks the grand climax of the process. It is at one and the same time the most complete testament of humanist learning in England, the fullest expression of the artistic spirit of the Renaissance, the final monument of the English Reformation—in so far as Puritanism can be regarded as its logical outcome—and the only true epic in the English language, and one which makes other efforts in the same *genre* pale into insignificance.

Yet in spite of its greatness *Paradise Lost* is like a magnificent edifice that everybody admires from the outside but which few enter. As Dr Johnson said, its perusal is 'a duty rather than a pleasure'. The religious task that Milton had set himself—'things unattempted yet in Prose or Rhime'—was one of incredible difficulty. His aim was not a narrative one, as in Homer and Virgil. Nor was it a narrative exposition of a theological system, as in Dante's *Divina Commedia*. It was, Milton says, 'to justify the ways of God to Man'—but this apparently simple purpose involved theological and philosophical considerations of the utmost complexity. It meant for example the exploration of the workings of Divine Providence, of the nature of evil, of the hope of redemption, and of the preparation of men's hearts for the coming of the Holy Spirit. It is doubtful, moreover, whether Milton was working from any settled creed. On the contrary it is more than likely that he was working out all the doubts and confusions in his own mind and in that of his age, and all the intricacies of conflicting dogma and doctrine that accompanied them as he went along.

To his contemporaries, to those who thought and fought through the intellectual and physical battles of the age, these issues were of paramount importance. But to a large extent they went down to defeat with the Commonwealth. To the men of the Restoration, apart from the survivors such as Milton, and to those of the succeeding age with their search for order and balance and their entirely different theological temper, they had little appeal—and the kind of religious thinking and feeling that lay behind Milton's great work was never to revive. In the modern world full participation in *Paradise Lost* is almost impossible, for it assumes a background of learning and interests that no longer exists. In many ways *Paradise Lost* is more remote to us now than the *Iliad* of Homer and by comparison the world of Shakespeare seems thoroughly contemporary.

Shakespeare plays create this effect because of the warmth and concreteness of their humanity. Fundamentally Milton's preoccupation was no less humane. It would certainly be wrong to think of him as aloof from the issues he portrayed. There was both passion and tragic conflict in his own life and character and often these provide the main motive force in his work. Nevertheless Milton's personality lacks the inclusive humanity of Shakespeare's. As Wordsworth wrote of him: 'Thy soul was like a star, and dwelt apart'. As he grew older Milton's high conception of his duty as poet and Puritan, his ideas of seriousness, restraint, and religious decorum hardened, so that his verse lost much of its earlier sensuousness and variety and became an instrument as Olympian as its creator.

The blank verse of *Paradise Lost*, with its stately tread and stylistic devices that make it at times closer to Latin than English, is also something that 'dwells apart'. It is great in its own right, but it is not in the mainstream of the English poetic tradition. Its influence, moreover, like that of Spenser's *The Faerie Queene* has in the main been an unfortunate one. 'Our language', Joseph Addison declared in 1712, 'sunk under him', and Dr Johnson wrote of 'the Chinese Wall of Milton's blank verse'. It was so stamped with its creator's austere personality that those who

59

tried to learn from it usually became hollow imitators, as John Keats discovered when, prompted by a sound instinct of poetic self-preservation, he abandoned the writing of *Hyperion* because it was 'too Miltonic'.

None of this, of course, alters the fact that Milton is one of the greatest English poets. He lived and wrote at a point in our history when the worlds of the Middle Ages, the Renaissance, and the Puritan Revolution came into conflict—and fused in his verse. Whatever its other limitations, therefore, it is an essential medium for entering into the cultural, religious, and political reality of the times.

English prose in the seventeenth century still had a serious competitor in Latin. Bacon's *Instauratio Magna* and two of Hobbes's most important works were for example written in Latin. Robert Burton used English for the *Anatomy of Melancholy* only at his publisher's insistence, and, as late as 1647, Sir Thomas Browne chose his native language for *Pseudodoxia Epidemica* only on second thoughts. Latin was still the language for international controversy and during the Commonwealth and Protectorate in particular a vast amount was written in Latin—notably by John Milton as Latin Secretary (assisted after his blindness by Andrew Marvell). The influence of Latin upon English prose style, therefore, was considerable.

Nevertheless it was in the field of prose that some of the most revolutionary literary developments of the period took place. It is true that typically Elizabethan prose continued to be written. The tradition of Hakluyt, for example, still survived and writers like William Prynne continued the line of Puritan invective initiated by such Elizabethan writers as Philip Stubbes. The Elizabethan fictional tradition still flourished: the romances of Nicholas Breton and John Ford, for example, were natural successors to Lodge's *Rosalind*. There were outstanding examples of the short-story *genre* in Thomas Dekker's *The Wonderful Yeare*—which also anticipated Defoe's *Journal of the Plague Year*—and Greene's tracts on the London underworld are recalled in *Belman of London*.

Dekker's greatest prose work, however, *Gul's Horn-Booke* (1609) is an important link between old and new. Through its indirect debt to Erasmus it has contacts with the medieval and early Tudor allegorical tradition, but its realistic caricature is more sharply controlled than that of the Elizabethan writers, and closer to the method of Ben Jonson in his realistic comedies. It

60

Original articles of agreement dated 27 April 1667 between John Milton, gentleman, and Samuel Symons, printer, for the sale of the copyright of 'A Poem entitled "Paradise Lost" '

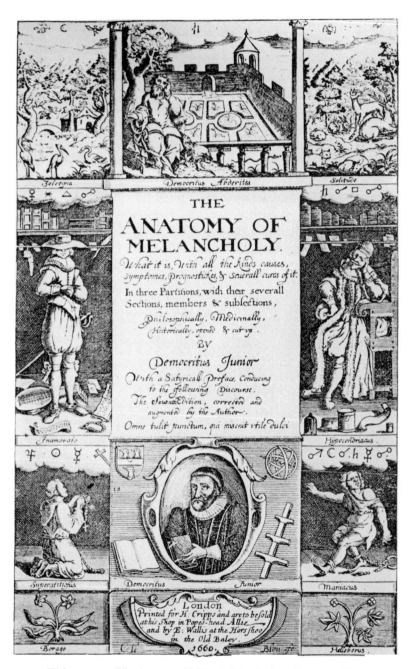

Title-page to *The Anatomy of Melancholy* by Robert Burton, 1660

points forward, moreover, to the eighteenth-century humorists, especially to Steele, Swift, and Addison.

The *Gul's Horn-Booke* was also close in method to the collections of 'Characters', the most notable of which were those published under the name of Sir Thomas Overbury in 1614 (though many of the sketches were by other hands) and the *Microcosmographie* of John Earle. The isolation of types in these writings to some extent indicated a more specialized or departmentalized attitude towards life, similar to that already noted in the plays of Webster which contained many 'Character' sketches to the detriment of characterization in a profounder sense—and it is significant that Webster was almost certainly one of the contributors to the Overbury collection. On the other hand the compactness of these little pieces and their pointed and economical style provided a useful discipline and their approach involved a heightening of objective observation which pointed forward to the essays of Addison and Steele and to some extent to the eighteenth-century novelists.

The 'fantastick' writers constitute another group which, in retrospect at any rate, seem typical of the seventeenth century. One of the first was Thomas Coryat, author of *Coryat's Crudities, hastily gobbled up in Five Months' Travels in France, Savoy, Italy, Rhetia, Helvetia, High Germany, and the Netherlands* (1611). Coryat was in some respects a descendant of early Tudor jesters, but there is a deliberate whimsicality in his approach which might almost be called 'journalistic'—he even had his 'gimmick', for he made his travels in one pair of shoes which he afterwards hung up in the parish church of Odcombe in Somerset, 'my dear natalitiall place'.

The 'fantastick' vein was closely allied to the 'melancholick', as in Burton's famous book whose full title is itself sufficient indication of the whimsical approach: *The Anatomy of Melancholy: What It Is. With all the Kindes, Causes, Symptoms, Prognostickes, and severall Cures of it. In three Maine Partitions with their severall Sections, Members and Subsections, Philosophically, Medicinally, Historically, opened and cut up. By Democritus Junior. With a Satyricall Preface Conducing to the following Discourse: Macrob. 'Omne meum, Nihil meum.'*

The book is an enormous repository of classical, medieval, and contemporary lore on Burton's chosen subject. It is in essence a picture of human folly, and as such it is related to classical satirists such as Lucian, to fifteenth and sixteenth-century satirical works, and also to the work of Rabelais and Montaigne.

61

But what marks it out as a characteristic product of the period is the pervading presence of the author's personality, a conscious distillation which was rare among earlier writers.

A similar mixture of whimsicality and pedantry is apparent in a number of other writers of the period—as for instance in Sir Thomas Urquhart of Cromarty the titles of whose books—like *Pantochronocanon* and *Logopandecteision*—give a fair idea of the idiosyncratic turn of his mind and style. Thomas Fuller's *Worthies* combined shrewd observation and 'fantastick' disquisitions, and the fashion also touched Sir Izaak Walton's charming adaptation of Elizabethan pastoral, *The Compleat Angler*.

In many respects Sir Thomas Browne is related to the 'fantastick' group, and he too plays with 'melancholy'. In him, however, the sense of personality is even more strongly marked. In *Religio Medici*, for example, personality is a carefully cultivated part of his literary stock-in-trade, and he takes his reader into his confidence, inviting him to admiration for his learning, amused indulgence for his foibles and eccentricities, and awe in the face of his perorations. The 'I' of literature is beginning to take on a new importance and 'the dear reader' is on the way.

To some extent the exploitation of personality together with the new self-consciousness that was its product was one of the symptoms of the seventeenth-century crisis of humanism—a frantic thrusting upwards of the self in a period when old traditions and sanctions were being threatened. At the same time it was also a preparation both for the psychological explorations of the novel and ultimately for the literature of self-revelation that was to be an outstanding feature of the Romantic Revival.

There were indeed other signs pointing in the same direction. There was the increase in biography, often of an informal and intimate nature, as in Izaak Walton's delightful *Lives*, perhaps the first true biographical essays in English literature. Allied to biography was the reporting of conversations, as in the *Table Talk* of John Selden. Autobiographical writings too became increasingly frequent, though these mostly circulated in manuscript. The most natural in style (and credible in content) was Cowley's *Essay of Myself*, contained among the papers left behind at his death in 1672. Private diaries too began to be compiled—notably those of the Presbyterian Richard Baxter and of the Quaker George Fox—while the letters of Dorothy Osborne to William Temple embodied her belief that 'all letters . . . should be as free and easy as one's discourse'.

The 'fantastick' vein was closely related to the 'Metaphysical'. Burton's *Anatomy of Melancholy* for example contains instances of paradoxical wit of the type associated with the 'Metaphysicals', and Browne, in *The Garden of Cyrus*, explores his ideas in all their associations with the same tenacity and ingenuity that Donne employed in some of his most characteristic poems.

Donne indeed is the pre-eminent exponent of the 'Metaphysical' manner in prose as well as in poetry. In *Paradoxes and Problems*, his earliest prose work, contemporaneous with the early poems, he fastens upon a theme and conducts elaborate five-finger exercises upon it much as he does in the lighter of the love poems. It is noteworthy, however, that even in this early work there is greater passion and urgency in Donne's prose than in that of Browne. This is evident above all in his *Sermons*, which constitute some of the finest prose of the period.

In Browne's magnificent peroration in *Hydriotaphia, or Urne Buriall* Latinisms, Biblical echoes, the rhythmical balance of the clauses and their careful unfolding create a deliberate, architectonic effect, as of a lofty vault filled with reverberating echoes. But the very deliberation produces a certain distancing of the emotion, so that the funerary urns which inspired it take on the nature of a 'literary occasion'.

In Donne's great sermons, on the other hand, he *experiences* his theme as he goes along, in the mind and 'on the pulses', in all its exact sensuous connotations. Ideas, theories, doctrines, quotations, allusions, images, and conceits are all devoted to this end: they are inherent, caught up in the intensity of the emotion. This unity of thought and feeling, content and manner, was more characteristic of Tudor prose than that of the seventeenth century, and Donne's *Sermons* are still close both to Tudor and medieval traditions. Their method, too, was medieval, founded on syllogistic reasoning with frequent appeals to authority, and their theology was to a large extent a continuation of the ideas of St Augustine and St Thomas Aquinas.

At the same time Donne, like the medieval and Tudor preachers, drives home his theological argument by means of the sensuous language and imagery of common speech.

To some extent this is merely to say that Donne's character and experience were different from Browne's and that his genius was more powerful and comprehensive. But the difference between the two writers is also symptomatic of a change in the attitude of many seventeenth-century writers, a change which became more marked as the century progressed. In Tudor prose there had been little differentiation of function, because there had been no over-riding necessity for it. It had been at one and the same time the prose of narrative, description, controversy, sensation, and emotion. Its appeal was usually directed simultaneously to the intellect and the senses—with the senses predominant. In the seventeenth century however a split in the various functions of prose *did* begin to make itself felt. It is not evident in Donne's prose—but the way in which Browne's finest passages tend to be 'set pieces', separate from rather than springing out of their con-text, together with the curious sometimes dilettante attitude of mind behind them, in some respects illustrates this split.

It was of course inevitable, because prose was being called upon to undertake new tasks. Above all there was the need for a medium better suited than the poetic and often chaotic prose of the Tudors to rational argument and exposition, and on the whole the trend of seventeenth-century prose was increasingly towards an emphasis upon matter rather than manner.

This shift of emphasis is underlined by the change in Latin models. For the Elizabethans the ideal had been Cicero, and their chief aim therefore had been amplification and embellishment. It is true that Milton tended to prefer the Ciceronian style but many of the seventeenth-century writers, in their desire for more con-centration and weight, preferred the epigrammatic terseness of Seneca or Tacitus. Especially evident in the *Essays* of Sir Francis Bacon, this influence was also partly responsible for the neatness and economy of the 'Character' writers. It is apparent, too, in Browne's *Religio Medici* and occasionally even in Burton's *Anatomy of Melancholy*, while the sermons of Lancelot Andrewes combine 'Metaphysical' wit with the terseness and pointed antithesis of the Latin writers.

In spite of the religious passions of the period, indeed, there was a growing trend in theological prose in the direction of clear and logical argument. Even the heat of controversy could at times produce a rational and moderate approach, as in the anti-Episcopalian tract *Smectymnuus*, and, among the group known as the 'Cambridge Platonists', Ralph Cudworth and Benjamin Whichcote also showed the growing tendency towards clarity and directness of expression.

For the most part, too, the political discussion of the period led to a plainer prose concentrating on logical exposition and argu-ment. The comprehensive and tightly argued nature of Hobbes's

64

theme in his *Leviathan* also demanded a strong and unadorned style, concerned more with matter than manner and rejecting some of the emotional qualities of language in favour of lucidity.

These changes were closely related to the growing need for a kind of prose better suited to scientific speculation and investigation. The scientific spirit indeed was present in a number of the prose writers already mentioned—and, if it comes to that, had existed also in the Elizabethan period. For example, although Burton's book was largely medieval in attitude and completely lacking in scientific method, it did contain an understanding of human psychology together with genuine observation and some scientific curiosity. Browne, too, recognized the need of referring popular superstition to the test of experiment and came close to recognizing the need for a distinction between the field of scientific inquiry and religious belief. The rational, humane tone of *Religio Medici* was also symptomatic of the new approach.

It was one thing, however, to register awareness of the spirit of scientific inquiry, another to find a way of expression that would approximate to it. This was in essence the great achievement of Sir Francis Bacon. Though he was not himself a scientist—and his works contain a number of the same kind of extravagancies and superstitions that occur in Browne's or Burton's books—he was the first to advocate, energetically and consistently, a radical change in intellectual approach and attitude whereby direct observation and experiment would take precedence over abstract speculation, so that man could achieve mastery over the material world.

His conception of language was subordinated to this great task. His prose style, although it has not lost the concrete force of popular speech, is largely different in intention to that of the Elizabethans. This is particularly noticeable in his use of imagery. Whereas in Elizabethan prose similes and metaphors were used for the most part to increase the emotional effect and to heighten muscular sensation, in Bacon they are present rather as lawyer's devices—as forensic *illustrations*.

His utilitarian attitude is clearly brought out in Book II of *The Advancement of Learning* (1605) where he attaches the greatest value to those functions of language which are related to exact observation and analysis. He deplores rhetorical devices as mere 'ornament' and he describes images as useful mainly 'to clothe and adorn' concrete ideas. When he deals with poetry his tributes tend to be conventional and disengaged and he leaves little doubt that as far as he is concerned the imagination must be regarded as

65

a lesser activity of the human mind, and imaginative writing inferior to the descriptive and analytical.

The intention behind Bacon's style was very close to that of the new Royal Society for the Advancement of Learning (founded in 1660—though a nucleus had existed before that), as defined by its historian Thomas Sprat: 'to separate the knowledge of Nature from the colours of Rhetorick, the devices of Fancy or the delightful deceit of Fables' so that mankind could achieve 'a dominion over *Things*'.

This separation of functions pioneered by Bacon inevitably had some adverse effects. It carried the possible implication that the kind of language he advocated was the only serious vehicle for human thought and endeavour, while that of the imagination was fanciful and remote from the important issues of life. It created a gulf between the scientist and the artist, tending to encourage the scientist on the one hand to ignore the insights provided by the artist, and the artist on the other to withdraw to an Ivory Tower. The gulf was to become wider as time went by, with serious consequences for the spiritual and cultural life of our own times. But without it scientific advance would have been impossible, and although prose such as Donne wrote, with its fusing of thought, feeling, and imagination, became rarer, the new influences led to a release of fresh energies and a whole new range of subject-matter.

There is, in any case, another great body of English prose still to be considered, which represents one of the most vital and durable of all the English literary traditions.

The Bible of 1611—the Authorized Version—was the work of forty-seven scholars nominated by James I and presided over by Bishop Lancelot Andrewes. The compilers set out to find a language which would be simple, homely, and vivid at the same time that it was lofty and reverent. In this they were helped by the work of the earlier translators. They rejected the more archaic of their renderings, but retained those words, turns of phrase, and grammatical usages which, whether current or not, seemed to them to have kept their clarity and force. The result was an amalgam of their own renderings and the best elements in the versions of Wyclif, Tyndale, and Coverdale—a kind of 'biblical dialect' which was not the same as everyday speech past or present, but which drew from it its freshness and strength, and in the process took on a timeless quality ideally suited to the universal nature of the material.

At the King's command this Bible was appointed to be read in all the churches, and it was also adopted by the Puritans in preference to the 'Geneva Bible'. For nearly three hundred years indeed it was accepted almost without question by all the Protestant sects and for much of that time it circulated among all classes and was the daily reading of the whole nation. Its influence therefore was enormous. In one way or another it affected the practice of most of the writers of the period and of the years that followed. It represented an ideal of vigour, dignity, and lucidity for the bookish and the learned—and for the unlearned it provided a complete education in itself. Above all it helped a wandering tinker and preacher to write a book which was to become its closest rival in popularity.

The great works of John Bunyan were written after the Restoration, but in spirit they belonged to the Puritan Revolution and the Commonwealth. The Bible was not in fact the only influence behind them, though it was the most important. Bunyan's allegory has obvious affinities with the Middle Ages. It has already been noted, for example, that *The Pilgrim's Progress* begins—like Langland's *Piers Plowman*—with a dream, and it also inherits the tradition of the Miracle and Morality Plays. Behind it too were many earlier allegories on similar lines, which had long been familiar to the popular mind.

None of these indeed were influences in the purely literary sense. For Bunyan's work grew out of popular culture. It was, for instance, closely related to a long line of popular preachers who drew their illustrations, imbued with practical experience and folk-wisdom, from everyday life. His language and imagery derived much of its force from the vigour, humour, and raciness of common speech, which had formed the basis of the Tudor Jest Books, the Elizabethan pamphlets, and much of the dialogue of the great plays. There was also behind him a whole host of forgotten Puritan pamphleteers and 'mechanick preachers' of 'the true old Enthusiastick Breed'. And it was the blending of all these popular traditions with the dignity of the biblical tradition that gave Bunyan's style much of its beauty and strength.

The blending itself of course was the product of genius and no account of the separate elements can begin to do justice to its originality. Bunyan indeed has the gifts of the born story-teller. He is a natural master of variations of pace and mood and of light and shade. His scenes and characters are realized with a wealth of realistic detail, and his ear for dialogue is as acute as that of the great dramatists. In consequence characters such as Mr By-Ends and Mr Worldly Wiseman, in spite of their allegorical labels, become living, three-dimensional people. Indeed the names that Bunyan chose are so charged with moral and emotional associations that they are, in themselves, something more than flat counters.

Bunyan's primary intention of course was not that of the novelist. His choice of the narrative form, like Milton's choice of epic for *Paradise Lost*, was entirely subordinate to the religious and spiritual intention. His aim in writing *The Pilgrim's Progress* was to lead men and women into the way of salvation by means of a simple parable, a kind of Christian fairy-tale. But in the process he undoubtedly anticipated the novel, while his analysis of spiritual conflict in *Grace Abounding to the Chief of Sinners* looked forward both to the psychological fiction of the future and to the literature of personal confession.

In surveying the prose of this transitional period therefore its two greatest exponents must be placed side by side, for to a large extent they complement each other. The great pioneer of the scientific movement gave to men's attitude to life and therefore to their style of writing, entirely new directions. The author of *The Pilgrim's Progress* proved that the language of the common people —the 'language really used by men'—was still healthy and active. Bacon's prose was the prose of the intellect and of the reason: Bunyan's was the prose of the imagination and the intuitions, refined and purified by the influence of the Bible. Bacon's prose was a necessary instrument of the new philosophical and scientific theories: Bunyan's was the guarantee that the life of the imagination and the spirit still persisted.

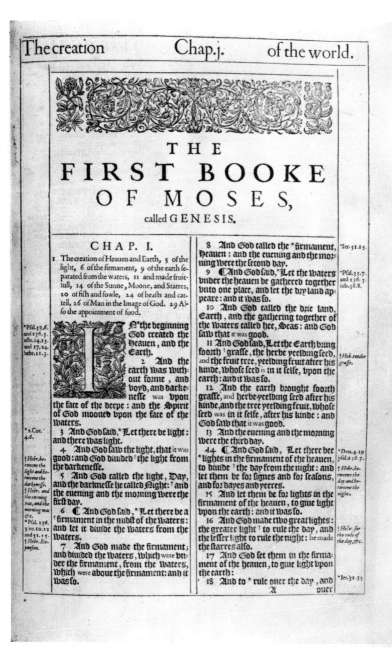

THE
FIRST BOOKE
OF MOSES,
called GENESIS.

CHAP. I.

1 The creation of Heauen and Earth, 3 of the light, 6 of the firmament, 9 of the earth separated from the waters, 11 and made fruitfull, 14 of the Sunne, Moone, and Starres, 20 of fish and fowle, 24 of beasts and cattell, 26 of Man in the Image of God. 29 Also the appointment of food.

*Psal.33.6. and 136.5. acts.14.15. and 17.24. hebr.11.3.

I**N** the beginning God created the Heauen, and the Earth.

2 And the earth was without forme, and voyd, and darkenesse was vpon the face of the deepe: and the Spirit of God mooued vpon the face of the waters.

*2.Cor. 4.6.

3 And God said,*Let there be light: and there was light.

†Hebr.betweene the light and betweene the darkenesse.
†Hebr. and the euening was, and the morning was &c.
*Psal. 136. 5.ier.10.12 and 51.15. †Hebr. Expansion.

4 And God saw the light, that it was good: and God diuided †the light from the darkenesse.

5 And God called the light, Day, and the darkenesse he called Night: † and the euening and the morning were the first day.

6 ¶ And God said,* Let there be a firmament in the midst of the waters: and let it diuide the waters from the waters.

7 And God made the firmament; and diuided the waters, which were vnder the firmament, from the waters, which were aboue the firmament: and it was so.

8 And God called the *firmament, Heauen: and the euening and the morning were the second day.

*Ier.51.15.

9 ¶ And God said,*Let the waters vnder the heauen be gathered together vnto one place, and let the dry land appeare: and it was so.

*Psal.33.7. and 136.5. iob.38.8.

10 And God called the drie land, Earth, and the gathering together of the waters called hee, Seas: and God saw that it was good.

11 And God said, Let the Earth bring foorth † grasse, the herbe yeelding seed, and the fruit tree, yeelding fruit after his kinde, whose seed is in it selfe, vpon the earth: and it was so.

†Heb.tender grasse.

12 And the earth brought foorth grasse, and herbe yeelding seed after his kinde, and the tree yeelding fruit, whose seed was in it selfe, after his kinde: and God saw that it was good.

13 And the euening and the morning were the third day.

14 ¶ And God said, Let there bee *lights in the firmament of the heauen, to diuide †the day from the night: and let them be for signes and for seasons, and for dayes and yeeres.

*Deu.4.19 psal.136.7.
†Hebr.betweene the day and betweene the night.

15 And let them be for lights in the firmament of the heauen, to giue light vpon the earth: and it was so.

16 And God made two great lights: the greater light † to rule the day, and the lesser light to rule the night: he made the starres also.

†Heb. for the rule of the day,&c.

17 And God set them in the firmament of the heauen, to giue light vpon the earth:

18 And to * rule ouer the day, and ouer

*Ier.31.35.

A

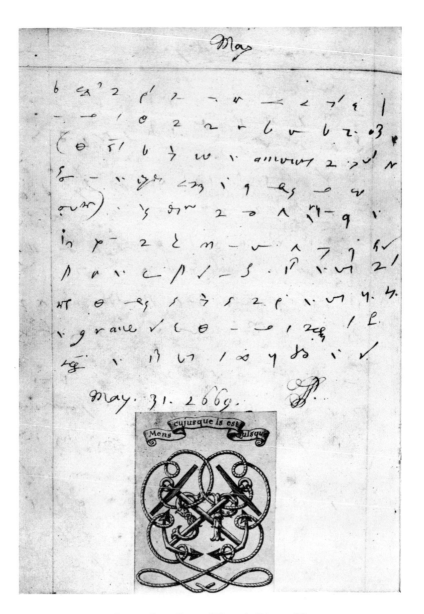

A page from Samuel Pepys's *Diary*, 1669

4 · The Age of Prose

SOME preliminary justification is needed for describing the period of English literature which stretches from the Restoration to the dawn of the Romantic Revival, and which includes such great poets as Pope and Dryden, as an 'age of prose'. The term, however, does contain a good deal of the truth. While poetry certainly extended its frontiers to incorporate new experiences and emotions, it was prose that occupied the greatest areas of territory.

In a literature, moreover, that was first and foremost one of social record, the poetry itself was imbued with the spirit of prose. This does *not* mean that it was prosaic, or lacking in its own special kind of beauty. As T. S. Eliot has pointed out, 'to have the virtues of good prose is the first and minimum requirement of good poetry', and great poetry can be made out of the ingredients of prose. John Donne, for example, created some of his most passionate effects out of a learned but fundamentally colloquial dialogue, and it was only his lesser imitators who turned the manner into a clogged and lifeless convention. The great achievement of John Dryden's poetry was, T. S. Eliot says, 'to cleanse the language of verse and once more bring it back to the prose order. For this reason, he was a great poet.' And towards the end of the eighteenth century when poetry had once more become false and stilted William Wordsworth set himself a similar task (though of course with an entirely different emphasis) when he insisted that poetry must be brought back to 'the language really used by men'.

This prevalence of the spirit of prose was related to the political, social, and economic events of the period and to the various currents of thought and feeling that lay behind them. When the monarchy was restored in 1660 men's deepest desire was for peace, stability, and the avoidance of political extremes—together with the passions that produce them. It is true that Charles II returned as an absolute monarch, and that the triumphant Royalists were not remiss in exacting vengeance. But the population were in no mood for a further prolonged blood-bath. There were, in fact, some surprising instances of political toleration, some of them extending to literature. Although Samuel Butler's mock-heroic poem *Hudibras* with its savage lampooning of Presbyterians and

Independents gave expression to the 'accepted' Restoration point of view, there were no attempts to suppress Milton's *Samson Agonistes*, which in another age might well have been regarded as 'subversive literature', and other supporters of the Commonwealth, including Milton's old colleague Andrew Marvell, continued to write anti-Royalist satires.

The nature of the restored monarchy differed widely from what it had been in Tudor and Early Stuart times. This was not only due to the relaxed character of the King and his court. Although there is no doubting the boisterous and impudent vitality with which court comedy in the hands of such practitioners as Sir George Etherege, William Wycherley, William Congreve, and Sir John Vanbrugh irrupted upon the stages of the reopened theatres, as if determined to exorcize every memory both of exile and the long twilight of Puritan joylessness, there is in its indecencies an element almost of desperation. For it was in large part a reassertion of a right to unfettered enjoyment, to an aristocratic self-sufficiency and irresponsibility, that were no longer in tune with the times. It was, moreover, court drama—isolated from the underlying predilections of the vast majority and particularly from those of the growing middle classes.

It was perhaps an intuitive appreciation of the isolation, and inevitable transience of the ethos of the Restoration court that lay behind the tempestuous career of the most considerable as well as one of the most obscene of the court poets, John Wilmot, Earl of Rochester, which culminated in public conversion.

The restored monarchy may have been an absolutism, and after the long years of civil conflict the idea, receiving weighty support from the philosophy of Thomas Hobbes, was not at first repugnant. But what the majority wanted from the monarchy was that it should be a *practical* means of securing the conditions that would allow them to get on with their everyday affairs. It was monarchy soberly accepted, no longer attended by the dangerous and intemperate *mystique* of the 'Divine Right of Kings'—and it is likely that the King himself was well aware of the fact.

Even during the Restoration period, too, there were developments that pointed the way towards the evolution of a constitutional monarchy. There were, for example, the beginnings of the Cabinet system and the germs of a properly constituted Opposition, involving the ideal (if not the practice) of a rational give and take of argument and discussion. The tone of civilized reasonableness in Lord Halifax's political treatise *The Character of a Trimmer*

(1688) and the ideals it set forth—impartiality of the law, latitude in matters of faith, and a middle way between absolute monarchy and mob-republicanism—more or less summed up the deepest desires and convictions of the age.

The fact that compromise could be urged as an acceptable course of conduct was itself a measure of the growing distaste for extremes and the growing desire for order and balance. It is significant, too, that the age did in fact produce a number of notorious 'trimmers', whose political or religious acrobatics were accepted with a considerable degree of tolerance. Dryden's vacillations between the Church of England and the Church of Rome, for example, in the long run had little effect upon his reputation, and at least a measure of indulgence was extended to career politicians, without the advantages of noble birth or wealth behind them, who might find themselves caught on the wrong foot in their changes of allegiance. Although Matthew Prior was nearly impeached after the downfall of the Tories in 1714 for his share in the Peace of Utrecht he was in the event allowed to go into a peaceful retirement and the publication of his *Collected Poems* received financial backing from former political foes as well as from his friends.

The emergence of men of humble birth like Prior in responsible positions was indeed a further symptom of a more practical attitude towards government, and the Restoration had already witnessed what might be called the beginnings of a modern Civil Service, reflected in the career of Samuel Pepys whose famous *Diary* was compiled between the years 1660 and 1669.

Gradually the monarchy changed its nature until the Convention Parliament of 1689 settled the broad bases of the political system of the country upon what Edmund Burke was later to describe as 'that ancient constitution formed by the original contract of the British state'—by which he implied the careful balance of powers within the realm.

This system, it is true, did not evolve without violence, or without a frequent revival of political passions as intense and often as dangerous as those of the seventeenth century. There was Titus Oates's anti-Catholic Plot of 1678; there were the frantic attempts to block the succession of James II, and Shaftesbury's intrigues after he came to the throne (satirized in Dryden's *Absalom and Achitophel*); there was the Monmouth Rebellion of 1685 and its bloody suppression. Even after 'the Glorious Revolution' which placed William III on the throne ('our great restorer' as Locke called him) there were many serious crises. In the eighteenth century there were the anti-Dissenter riots, the violent Tory attacks on the Duke of Marlborough, in which Swift's *The Conduct of the Allies* (1711) substantially contributed to the hero's downfall. Serious political dissensions attended the accession of the Hanoverian line, and there were the Jacobite risings of the '15 and the '45. These and other crises brought the menacing shadow of civil conflict very close on more than one occasion—but the memories of the past and the deep-seated concern for social order that dominated the whole period from 1660 onwards, in the last resort always reasserted themselves and averted the final disaster.

The inclination towards restraint and tolerance received solid philosophical backing from the writings of John Locke, whose teachings, after the Glorious Revolution, largely displaced those of Hobbes. The second of Locke's *Two Treatises on Government* (1690), with its cogent exposition of the need for the balance of constitutional powers and the maintenance of the subject's rights, had a particularly profound influence upon the political thinking not only of his own country but in due course of all those other countries—including the United States of America—whose political systems derived from the British Constitution. And towards the end of the eighteenth century Locke's influence was powerfully supplemented by that of Edmund Burke, who, with his strong intuitive feeling for history and tradition, added an emotional (one might almost say 'Romantic') colour to Locke's lucid and rational approach—and who incidentally championed the American colonists whose own political ideals owed so much to Locke.

A similar trend away from passion and towards tolerance and reasonableness distinguishes the religion of the period. The old enthusiasm survived the Restoration: it was apparent in the great works of Bunyan, and in the writings of Thomas Ellwood and others. It was never completely extinguished, breaking out again, for example, in William Law's *A Serious Call to a Devout and Holy Life* (1728) which was one of the prose masterpieces of the age. Because of the influence of this work and that of his other mystical writings upon the brothers Wesley, Law has been called the 'father of Methodism'—and he is therefore a link between 'the old enthusiastick breed' and the return of religious inspiration that was one of the elements of the Romantic Revival.

As far as the restored Church of England was concerned, however, the preference of preachers and theologians such as Isaac Barrow, Robert South, and John Tillotson was for clarity and logical demonstration in matters of faith, with little concession to mysticism or exaltation—though they were not without flights of eloquence, in which biblical rhythms and echoes deepened their styles. After 1688, however, Anglicanism tended increasingly to become Low Church and latitudinarian in the spirit of rationalism.

The influence of Locke (though to some extent it was offset by that of Berkeley's idealist philosophy) was again important. He argued in various writings that religion was a matter of personal conscience which should be left free, in so far as it did not encroach upon the security of the State. He respected existing beliefs, deriving from the Bible a reasonable Christian teaching that eschewed mystery and was predominantly ethical in intent: 'our business here', he asserted, 'is not to know all things, but those which concern our conduct'—and this is a sentiment that echoed through much of the poetry and prose of the period.

Of all Locke's writings, however, it was *An Essay Concerning Human Understanding* (1690) that most comprehensively gave expression to, and helped to direct, the profoundest instincts of the age, besides being a major contribution to European philosophy. His approach in this great work is eminently practical and utilitarian. It is the rational mind that receives pride of place: he discards intuition, and he sees intelligence as the product merely of sensation and experience. He elevates judgment—which analyses and distinguishes ideas—over 'wit' (which in this context is very close to the imagination as it is understood today)—which unites them by resemblances.

Above all he is concerned for the clear definition of words and ideas, and his pleas for a more exact use of language (reinforced by the arguments of the French critics) had a tremendous influence upon the search by the writers of the period for 'correctness'.

Locke's essay also stimulated interest in psychological analysis of motive and behaviour—and the 'science of man' became a major preoccupation, finding expression in many literary works, and pre-eminently in Alexander Pope's *An Essay on Man*, besides indirectly affecting the psychological approach of novelists such as Samuel Richardson.

This stress upon exactness of expression, upon a clear equivalence of word and thing (amply demonstrated in Locke's own vigorous and lucid prose) reinforced the similar concern of Bacon in the seventeenth century and was directly related to the needs of the new science, which made great strides during the period. The Royal Society for Improving Natural Knowledge marked the culmination of the trend inaugurated by Bacon's *Instauratio Magna*.

73

English Literature

Many leading writers, including Cowley, Denham, Waller, Dryden, and the diarist Evelyn were members—and this close association between science and literature was itself a significant feature of the age, pointing to a fruitful union which, as science became more and more complex, was eventually to become impracticable.

At this stage, however, many of the great scientific figures must be included in a survey of the literature of the period because their work impinged upon the consciousness of its writers. Among them were John Wallis and Seth Ward the mathematicians, Edmund Halley the astronomer, the physicians and physiologists John Mayow, Thomas Sydenham, and Robert Boyle—and towering above them all Sir Isaac Newton, the discoverer of the laws of gravitation, of the decomposition of white light in the spectrum, and of the theory of fluxions. Newton's greatest scientific work was written in Latin, but he too could command a clear and sinewy English prose style, as in his *Opticks* which exercised a powerful imaginative appeal upon his generation.

The scientists were equally indebted to the writers, and particularly to Dryden. To some extent Dryden's prose was still transitional, retaining as it did a good deal of the raciness of the Jacobeans and Elizabethans, and indeed this could be said of much of the great prose of the period, including that of Jonathan Swift, until Joseph Addison set a somewhat different standard, more refined and urbane and adapted to the requirements of a wider public. At the same time, it was Dryden who purged English prose of its remaining archaisms and confusions, creating a medium for reasonable discourse, attentive to the opponent's point of view, as well as for philosophical and scientific exposition.

The scientific discoveries and theories of Newton and his fellows were, with the help of Locke's ideas, absorbed without difficulty into the concept of an ordered universe controlled by a beneficent deity, with man as His supreme creation. Indeed the demonstration of gravitation or of the nature of light, or of the wonders of microscopic biology, appeared to provide further and reassuring evidence of a universe magnificently intelligent in cause and effect.

The scholastic philosophy of the Middle Ages, and Elizabethan expositions such as Hooker's *The Laws of Ecclesiastical Politie*, had been equally confident in their assumption of God's laws directing every created thing according to its nature. The difference lay in the fact that whereas the earlier picture depended on the proofs of scholastic logic, now they seemed to rely rather upon the demonstrable proofs of scientific experiment. Faith seemed less a matter of taking the universe on trust than of investigating it and discovering more and more convincing and intellectually satisfying proofs of the divine order.

These confident conclusions, it is true, did not go altogether without challenge. There was Hobbes's largely mechanist philosophy; that of David Hume, more empirical than Locke's, came close to complete scepticism; and there were individuals who held agnostic views. But on the whole the period from 1660 until the ideas of the French *philosophes* began to make headway towards the end of the eighteenth century was, in its own restrained way, as much an age of faith as the Middle Ages themselves. Even the most extreme of the Deists never seriously doubted the existence of an Absolute establishing moral laws and requiring man to discover and obey them, if not by revelation then by reason.

This sublime confidence received characteristic expression in the lines of Pope's *An Essay on Man* which describe the divine harmony and culminate in the couplet:

> 'And spite of pride, in erring reason's spite,
> One truth is clear, Whatever is, is right.'

To modern ears this may sound chilly and complacent. But though Augustan religion may have lacked inspiration and enthusiasm it did not lack sincerity and conviction, and this is one respect in which the age, in spite of its modernity in so many others, is almost as remote from the twentieth century as the Middle Ages.

Within the somewhat narrow framework, moreover, there was more variety and depth of religious feeling than is sometimes allowed. Harsh personal experience, for example, made the religion of Dr Johnson and of William Cowper, though its basic assumptions may not have differed substantially from those of Pope, the reverse of complacent, inspiring some of Johnson's most sombrely impressive prose, and in the case of Cowper some of the most moving hymns in the language. Even the most tepid in their beliefs, moreover, generally subscribed to the Christian ethic, and though the period witnessed much cruelty and suffering (as Hogarth showed) there were also the beginnings of organized philanthropy, and on the whole the prevailing moral temper was one of practical humanism.

Both in politics and religion, therefore, the trend was away from the kind of emotional intensity that seeks its natural outlet in poetry and poetic drama, and towards the rational frame of mind that finds its appropriate level in prose or in literature close to the spirit of prose. Pepys's *Diary*, that unique account of the habits, prejudices, activities, and feelings—and indeed of the whole social ambience of the times—as observed by one singularly acute middle-class participant, conveys vividly the impression of a nation whose main concern was with the *practical* affairs of life. In this connexion it is important to note that London, even at this early stage (and especially after the Great Fire), emerges from the pages of the *Diary* as a capital rapidly transforming itself from a late medieval city into a great centre of commerce and finance. Before the end of the seventeenth century indeed many of the features of the modern business world had made their appearance. The Bank of England, for example, was founded in 1694 and five years before that Edward Lloyd had founded his famous coffee-house to which the business men and ship-owners of London thronged, and from which was to spring the greatest centre of maritime information and insurance in the world.

What Daniel Defoe called 'the grand affair of business' was in fact rapidly beginning to absorb many of the energies that had hitherto gone into religious and political dissension. The great economic expansion in town and country encouraged co-operation rather than disunity (the era of cut-throat competition had not yet arrived) and further strengthened the feeling of confidence in the 'rightness' of practical activity. The ugly scramble for riches that had horrified the moralists and satirists in the early years of the seventeenth century had to a considerable degree given way to orderly and organized effort. It was conceived, moreover, as effort that fitted into the whole scheme of things, and therefore to have received divine sanction, so that sober industry in the amassing of wealth became one of the Christian virtues and a sign of God's favour, to Nonconformists and Anglicans alike.

The new status of the business-man was soon reflected in literature. In the plays of Jonson and Massinger he had been depicted as a heartless miser, and this attitude lingered in Restoration comedy where he often appears as the rightful dupe of impudent and impecunious young gallants. The traders and merchants in Defoe's novels, or Sir Andrew Freeport in *The Spectator* are, on the other hand, represented as honourable and sympathetic figures.

The economic expansion affected the country as well as the towns. Farming methods were greatly improved and on the whole it was a period of agricultural prosperity, with a landed aristocracy

76

by and large interested in the betterment of their estates, a well-to-do squirearchy and yeomanry, much new building not only of great country-houses but also of manor-houses, farms, and parsonages, and the gradual emergence of a pattern of parkland, meadow, and hedgerow. There is, it is true, another side of the picture: the enclosure of the common lands, especially in the latter half of the eighteenth century, caused much misery among farm labourers, forcing many of them into the towns and depopulating many villages—a state of affairs reflected in Oliver Goldsmith's *The Deserted Village* and later in the poems of George Crabbe.

The attitude of most writers to the countryside, in marked contrast to that of the Romantics, was therefore controlled by purely practical considerations. It was the *products* of the land, not its scenic beauties, that excited Defoe, for example, in *A Tour thro' the Whole Island of Great Britain.*

The contemplation of the bounties of the countryside (even if they were exaggerated and idealized) inspired the same feeling of a God-ordained and orderly progress as that which attended developments in other spheres. It was a feeling that produced its own kind of passion. Pope's emotions, for example, as he describes the tasteless magnificence and pseudo-husbandry of 'Timon's' mansion in Epistle IV of *The Moral Essays* are certainly of a different kind from those of Wordsworth in the presence of the phenomena of wild Nature, but they are no less sincere. The spectacle of wanton extravagance and ostentation, because they are 'against Nature' in *his* sense of the term, moves him to profound moral indignation, in which is implicit a vision of Nature civilized by the hand of man:

> 'Another age shall see the golden ear
> Embrown the slope, and nod on the parterre,
> Deep harvests bury all his pride has planned,
> And laughing Ceres re-assume the land.'

This almost proprietary attitude towards the fruits of the earth and their nurture extended to most of the other activities of life. The literature of the age was very much a literature of *things*. Much of the excitement of Defoe's *The Life and Adventures of Robinson Crusoe* (1719), for example, comes from the detailed and loving catalogue of the stores and provisions (dear to any merchant heart) taken from the wreck, and from the description of Crusoe's ingenuity in adapting the natural resources of the island to his use. This kind of interest, of course, was not peculiar to the eighteenth century, and its presence in Defoe's famous novel is not sufficient by itself to explain its perennial appeal. That comes in part from the astonishing skill which endows both objects and situations with such concrete, and apparently artless, reality—a skill which is evident in most of Defoe's writings. In part, too, it springs from the fact that Robinson Crusoe is a symbol of man in his essence, man stripped of all social advantages, with only his will, his courage, and his faith to oppose to the buffetings of fortune. To some extent this is also the condition of the main characters in Defoe's other novels—of the hero of *Captain Singleton*, for example, and of the heroines of *Moll Flanders* and of *Roxana, the Fortunate Mistress*— but it is pre-eminently so of Robinson Crusoe. It was this quality that Coleridge stressed when he wrote of the novel: 'Defoe's excellence it is, to make me forget my specific class, character and circumstances, and to raise me, while I read him, into the universal man.'

What is certain, however, is that it was this period which, supported by the philosophical and scientific investigations of the day, placed so high a value upon the actual, the concrete, and the practical that formed the natural context for Defoe's achievement. The concern for 'things' in themselves, divorced from any extraneous aura of association or mystery, was in fact a general characteristic. There is, for example, the almost tangible realization of the objects on Belinda's dressing-table in Pope's *The Rape of the Lock*, and much of the charm of William Cowper's poetry derives from the presence of his beloved *Penates*. Even Dr Johnson who, from temperament and bitter personal experience, rejected materialistic values did so from the basis of a firm appreciation of them. There is, for example, a rich concreteness of reference in his poem *The Vanity of Human Wishes* and in his short poem *One and Twenty* with its sardonic invitation:

> 'Lavish of your grandsire's guineas,
> Show the spirit of an heir.'

The tendency was closely related to the fact that for these writers it was Man in society that was the ultimate standard of reference—even to those who like Defoe, or like Henry Fielding in *The Life of Jonathan Wild the Great*, placed him outside it. This was also one of the reasons why London so early on in the period came to occupy a pre-eminent place in the cultural life of the nation. There were other centres, and notably Bath in the west country, and there were the country-houses of the great, but it was in

London, men felt, that the social animal could best be studied in all his variety. Already in the pages of Pepys's *Diary* there is the sense of a capital city with its theatres, taverns, clubs, book-shops, and coffee-houses as the cultural Mecca of the most active minds of the age. It was in London, too, that 'taste' was formed. This was, throughout the period, the province of a small *élite*, whose main qualifications were social distinction, political importance, and classical learning. There were, however, important changes in the status of the writer. The patronage of the great was still for the majority the main avenue to success, and the system had its merits in so far as it brought the aristocracy and the world of letters into close contact to the benefit of both. But it could also be 'patronizing' in the worst sense of the word—as Dr Johnson knew only too well when in a famous letter to Lord Chesterfield he proudly declared his independence. Although Johnson's decision involved him in considerable penury for a time, other writers were more fortunate. The Copyright Act of 1709 improved their bargaining position, and the period witnessed some outstanding publishing successes, such as Pope's translations of the *Iliad* and of the *Odyssey*—dedicated significantly not to a noble patron but to a fellow-writer, William Congreve—which earned him a fortune.

These changes in the situation of the writer were related of course to the great expansion of the reading public, brought about by a number of factors, including the increased prosperity and security of the middle classes, the growth of circulating libraries and the improvements in roads and communications that made them possible, and (as far as the lower end of the middle-class scale was concerned) the spread of charitable foundations, Sunday schools, Dissenting academies, and, later on, the rise of Methodism. One of the consequences was the appearance in increasing numbers of periodicals designed to inform and educate the new public —and within the first two decades of the eighteenth century more than three hundred of them were launched. The majority were devoted to the small-talk of the London coffee-houses, but Sir Richard Steele and Joseph Addison had wider aims as well as a wider public in view. In *The Tatler* and then in the more famous *The Spectator* they set out to raise the tastes of their middle-class public by providing a regular commentary upon literature, philosophy, and the arts—and upon the values of civilized human behaviour in general. There was no question of vulgarizing taste, or of challenging the underlying assumption that its formation was in the hands of the specially qualified few. But both Steele and

Addison studied the needs of their audience and practised a simple urbane style. Addison's in particular was distinguished by its propriety, perspicuity, and elegance: it was, Dr Johnson declared, 'familiar but not coarse . . . elegant but not ostentatious'.

Other periodicals contained essays by Berkeley the philosopher, Johnson's 'Idler' essays, and Goldsmith's famous 'Citizen of the World' series. These periodicals, too, helped to foster that ideal of a civilized social unity which constitutes one of the chief characteristics of the age and one of its greatest strengths.

It was an ideal, moreover, that called forth some of its deepest feelings and some of its best writing, both in poetry and prose. To modern ears Pope's dictum 'the proper study of mankind is man' may not seem particularly inspiring, but to Pope and others like him it involved a profound concern for moral and cultural values. It was when he contemplated the possibility that these might be threatened that he was at his most eloquent, as in the closing lines of Book IV of *The Dunciad*:

> 'Lo! thy dread empire, Chaos is restor'd;
> Light dies before thy uncreating word:
> Thy hand, great Anarch! lets the curtain fall,
> And universal darkness buries all.'

All these factors—political, religious, economic, and social—directly or indirectly militated against extremes of feeling. In its literature, therefore, the age demanded modes that would unite, not divide, the nation. In private men might still experience intense passions, but they were expected to be mindful of their possible disruptive effects and not to display them in public, and if they were writers they were expected to keep the more personal of them out of their literature.

One of the consequences was the virtual disappearance of the personal lyric, as practised by the Elizabethans and Jacobeans. The court poets of the Restoration, it is true, exhibited some of the qualities of Caroline verse: the influence of Carew and Lovelace, for example, combined with that of Ben Jonson in the lyrics of Sir Thomas Sedley; and those of Thomas Sackville, Earl of Dorset, display a Caroline gaiety and badinage, and at the same time a neatness of syntax more in tune with the new tendencies. Something of the old magic lingers in their poems, and occasionally too in those of Rochester and Dryden and others.

The important point about most of these poets is, however, that they treat the lyric as something addressed to a general public rather than to an individual. It is a case of inviting a polite and civilized audience to a sharing of the surface elements of an experience, and not a passionate pouring forth of the emotions. In other words, it is *social* not personal utterance, lowered to the level of conversational style and prose sense—and this was the dominant tendency of all forms of English poetry from the Restoration to the beginnings of the Romantic Revival.

Within these limits, however, the lyric still achieved a considerable variety. The lyrical pieces of Matthew Prior, for example, are saved from conventionality because the Chloes and Lisettas to whom they are addressed had more than a nodding acquaintance with his own mistresses, so that there is wit and realism in many of them, as well as occasional tenderness. The ballad-opera verses of John Gay's *The Beggar's Opera* and ballad imitations such as Henry Carey's famous *Sally in Our Alley*, Oliver Goldsmith's *An Elegy on a Mad Dog*, and William Cowper's *The Ballad of John Gilpin* are by no means negligible. Patriotism, a 'public' and social emotion, and therefore acceptable, was reflected in Cowper's *The Loss of the Royal George*, David Garrick's *The Hearts of Oak*, James Thomson's *Rule Britannia*—and of course in the National Anthem itself. Conviviality too might be regarded as 'social', and there were such famous bucolic poems as *A Hunting We Will Go* and *The Roast Beef of Old England*.

Poets assumed a public *persona* even more readily when they came to write their more serious poems. Sometimes the result was a rhetoric that strikes modern ears as stilted and artificial, as if the poet had donned a full-bottomed wig to deliver it, while the accompanying ornamentations seem as chilly as the marble urns, busts, and canopies of the tombs in eighteenth-century churches. Dryden's *Annus Mirabilis, the Year of Wonders 1666* was one of the earlier examples, but a similar (if less decorated) rhetoric attends many other poems of the period—such as Pope's *Eloisa to Abelard* —and the conventions of this kind of poetry were accepted without discomfort by the public to which it was addressed. At times, too, and notably in Pope's *Elegy to the Memory of An Unfortunate Lady* where the manner is perfectly adapted to the subject and where private and public emotions have fused, the result could be impressive and moving. In Thomas Gray's *An Elegy in a Country Churchyard* the rhetoric is muted, but here too the tone is predominantly one of the social occasion.

For a poetry seeking to speak directly to a polite and civilized audience 'correctness' of expression was naturally a major preoccupation. It was no mere academic affectation, for it was directly related to the belief (supported by contemporary philosophy and science) that just as there was a 'correct' and divinely ordered universe, so there was a 'correct' and divinely ordered mode of human conduct which it was the duty of the poet to discover and portray. The call to 'follow Nature' therefore was a serious challenge to get as close as possible to these eternal truths —to find the words that would embody them clearly and un-ambiguously. The aim, Dryden declared, was 'deep thoughts in common language', and 'wit', though it stood for many things, usually implied an apprehension of the profound harmony of the universe combined with what Dr Johnson described as 'a propriety of words and thoughts adapted to the subject'. In these circum-stances literature was no dilettante activity: as Lord Mulgrave (later Duke of Buckingham) put it in *An Essay on Poetry*:

> 'Of all those arts in which the wise excel,
> Nature's chief masterpiece is writing well.'

It is the preoccupation with correctness of style that helps to explain the extraordinarily high—and as it was to seem to later critics, inflated—regard in which Edmund Waller and Sir John Denham were held, though most of their work was written before the Restoration. 'Methought', Waller is reported to have said, 'I never saw a good copy of English verses; they want smoothness; then I began to essay.' Although in fact 'Metaphysical' elements still linger in his verses, they are well controlled and smoothness does indeed attend them. To Restoration and eighteenth-century poets it seemed that he had 'essayed' to such purpose that he was the first really civilizing influence on English poetry. Dryden wrote of his use of rhyme that 'the excellence and dignity of it were never fully known till Mr Waller taught it: he first made writing easily an art', and this kind of tribute was applied both to Waller and Denham by many of the leading poets and critics of the day.

For Pope, Waller's 'sweetness' was supplemented by Denham's 'strength'. By 'strength' he chiefly had in mind Denham's handling of the couplet, particularly in *Cooper's Hill*, which, though it appeared as early as 1642, ranked in his estimation and in that of many of his contemporaries as the real starting-point of 'correct' poetic diction, and directly inspired Pope's own early descriptive poem *Windsor Forest*. The four lines (they are addressed to the River Thames) which Denham added to the 1653 edition of his poem became, indeed, a kind of aesthetic manifesto of Augustan intentions as regards style, content, and manner:

> 'O could I flow like thee, and make thy stream
> My great example, as it is my theme!
> Though deep, yet clear; though gentle, yet not dull;
> Strong without rage; without o'erflowing full.'

It was under the apprenticeship of these two earlier poets that Dryden placed himself. At first their influence had to compete with that of the 'Metaphysicals', and the poem which he wrote on the death of Oliver Cromwell, and its counter-piece—after he had changed his allegiance—on the return of Charles II both contained conceits as extravagant as any practised by Donne and his fellows, and there was still a good deal of strained imagery and language in *Annus Mirabilis*. But by the time he came to write his three great satires—*Absalom and Achitophel*, *The Medall: A Satyre Against Sedition*, and *MacFlecknoe*—his versification had absorbed all that Waller and Denham could teach and had developed into an instrument as flexible as it was precise.

Equally brilliant in technique though quite different in tone were the two religious poems, *Religio Laici* written in championship of the Church of England and *The Hind and the Panther*, written after his conversion to Roman Catholicism. Here the satirical elements are subsidiary and the versification is more that of polite and civilized discourse. One of Dryden's great contributions to the poetry of the age lay in fact in his demonstration of the scope and flexibility of the heroic couplet.

It is sometimes forgotten that it was only in the hands of the minor poets that this form of verse became stiff and mechanical. As practised by the major writers it encompassed an astonishing variety of mood and effect. There is the world of difference, for example, between Swift's racy doggerel and Charles Churchill's spluttering energy, or between Goldsmith's mellowness and Gay's light-hearted mockery. It is true that towards the end of the eighteenth century the heroic couplet tended to become clogged with epigrams and antitheses, but even so Johnson's vigorous and sombre satires, though not altogether free from these faults, gave further evidence of its poetic resources.

It is without question, however, the poetry of Pope that most fully demonstrated its vitality. He used it with equally telling effect for satire, mockery, badinage, diatribe, and narrative, and for a good many other purposes as well. He, more than any other poet of the period, achieved that completeness and finality of expression, that perfect correspondence between word and object ('What oft was thought, but ne'er so well express'd) which constituted the poetic ideal. He often did so, moreover, with effects of considerable beauty. There are, for example, the lines about Italy in Book IV of *The Dunciad* with their mellifluous alliteration:

> 'To isles of fragrance, lily-silver'd vales,
> Diffusing languor in the panting gales:
> To lands of singing, or of dancing slaves,
> Love-whispering woods, and lute-resounding waves.'

These lines probably represent the farthest point which Augustan poetry could reach as far as pure beauty is concerned, and they illustrate both its strength and its limitations. On the one hand, word, sound, and sense are perfectly related, and the effect aimed at has been triumphantly achieved. But on the other they leave little to the imagination: they are *too* accomplished, and the result is to finalize the reader's response, to bring it to a full stop. It lacks any penumbra of association, echo, or mystery—and it was for this reason that the poets of the Romantic Revival reacted against Pope and set out to explore those more intangible resources of the language which he and his contemporaries had neglected.

As literature was regarded so highly as a medium for uniting society and therefore for helping to fulfil the divine purpose, it followed that it must be perpetually kept up to the mark. Literary criticism in consequence enjoyed a particularly high status, and in an age which had a less exalted view of the poetic function than that which preceded or followed it, was considered a perfectly proper subject for poetry as well as for prose, and Pope's *An Essay on Criticism* represents the high-water mark of the *genre*.

The criticism of the period was shaped under the twin influences of classical and French writers. Horace's *Ars Poetica* was its aesthetic bible: there were several translations or imitations and many of the general critical ideas derived from it. The influence of the classics indeed upon every department of literature cannot be too strongly stressed—and in this respect the age was still closely linked with the Renaissance and Humanism. For this reason it has often been labelled the 'Classical Age': the other common description of 'Augustan' was almost certainly derived from Johnson's tribute to Dryden: '. . . What was said of Rome, adorned by Augustus, may be applied by an easy metaphor to English poetry embellished by Dryden . . . he found it brick, and he left it marble.'

THE
DUNCIAD,
VARIORVM.
WITH THE
PROLEGOMENA of *SCRIBLERUS*.

DEFEROR IN VICVM

VENDENTEM THVS ET ODORES

LONDON.
Printed for A. Dob . 1729.

Title-page to *The Dunciad* by Alexander Pope, 1729

The TATLER.

By *Isaac Bickerstaff* Esq;

Quicquid agunt Homines nostri Farrago Libelli.

Tuesday, April 12. 1709.

THO' the other Papers which are publish'd for the Use of the good People of England have certainly very wholesome Effects, and are laudable in their particular Kinds, they do not seem to come up to the main Design of such Narrations, which, I humbly presume, should be principally intended for the Use of Politick Persons, who are so publick-spirited as to neglect their own Affairs to look into Transactions of State. Now these Gentlemen, for the most Part, being Persons of strong Zeal and weak Intellects, It is both a Charitable and Necessary Work to offer something, whereby such worthy and well-affected Members of the Commonwealth may be instructed, after their Reading, what to think: Which shall be the End and Purpose of this my Paper, wherein I shall from Time to Time Report and Consider all Matters of what Kind soever that shall occur to Me, and publish such my Advices and Reflections every Tuesday, Thursday, and Saturday, in the Week, for the Convenience of the Post. It is also resolv'd by me to have something which may be of Entertainment to the Fair Sex, in Honour of whom I have taken the Title of this Paper. I therefore earnestly desire all Persons, without Distinction, to take it in for the present Gratis, and hereafter at the Price of one Penny, forbidding all Hawkers to take more for it at their Peril. And I desire all Persons to consider, that I am at a very great Charge for proper Materials for this Work, as well as that before I resolv'd upon it, I had settled a Correspondence in all Parts of the Known and Knowing World; and forasmuch as this Globe is not trodden upon by mere Drudges of Business only, but that Men of Spirit and Genius are justly to be esteem'd as considerable Agents in it, we shall not upon a Dearth of News present you with musty Foreign Edicts, or dull Proclamations, but shall divide our Relation of the Passages which occur in Action or Discourse throughout this Town, as well as elsewhere, under such Dates of Places as may prepare you for the Matter you are to expect, in the following Manner:

All Accounts of Gallantry, Pleasure, and Entertainment, shall be under the Article of White's Chocolate-house; Poetry, under that of Will's Coffee-house; Learning, under the Title of Grecian; Foreign and Domestick News, you will have from St. James's Coffee-house; and what else I shall on any other Subject offer, shall be dated from my own Apartment.

I once more desire my Reader to consider, That as I cannot keep an Ingenious Man to go daily to Will's, under Twopence each Day merely for his Charges; to White's, under Sixpence; nor to the Grecian, without allowing him some Plain Spanish, to be as able as others at the Learned Table; and that a good Observer cannot speak with even Kidney at St. James's without clean Linnen. I say, these Considerations will, I hope, make all Persons willing to comply with my Humble Request (when my Gratis Stock is exhausted) of a Penny a Piece; especially since they are sure of some Proper Amusement, and that it is impossible for me to want Means to entertain 'em, having, besides the Helps of my own Parts, the Power of Divination, and that I can, by casting a Figure, tell you all that will happen before it comes to pass.

But this last Faculty I shall use very sparingly, and not speak of any Thing 'till it is pass'd, for fear of divulging Matters which may offend our Superiors.

White's Chocolate-house, April 7.

THE deplorable Condition of a very pretty Gentleman, who walks here at the Hours when Men of Quality first appear, is what is very much lamented. His History is, That on the 9th of *September*, 1705. being in his One and twentieth Year, he was washing his Teeth at a Tavern Window in *Pall-Mall*, when a fine Equipage pass'd by, and in it a young Lady who look'd up at him; away goes the Coach, and the young Gentleman pull'd off his Night-Cap, and instead of rubbing his Gums, as he ought to do, out of the Window till about Four a Clock, he sits him down, and spoke not a Word till Twelve at Night; after which, he began to enquire, If any Body knew the Lady — The Company ask'd, What Lady? But he said no more, till they broke up at Six in the Morning. All the ensuing Winter he went from Church to Church every Sunday, and from Play-house to Play-house all the Week, but could never find the Original of the Picture which dwelt in his Bosom. In a Word, his Attention to any Thing, but his Passion, was utterly gone. He has lost all the Money he ever play'd for, and been confuted in every Argument he has enter'd upon since the Moment he first saw her. He is of a Noble Family, has naturally a very good Air, is of a frank, honest Temper: But this Passion has so extremely maul'd him, that his Features are set and uninform'd, and his whole Visage is deaden'd by a long Absence of Thought. He never appears in any Alacrity, but when rais'd by Wine; at which Time he is sure to come hither, and throw away a great deal of Wit on Fellows, who have no Sense further than just to observe, That our poor Lover has most Understanding

The classical influence, however, was not confined to that of the writers of the age of Augustus Caesar. In criticism Aristotle and Longinus enjoyed reputations at least equal to that of Horace, and in literature Homer was the ultimate genius and standard of reference before whom every other writer paled into insignificance. Classical quotations and allusions abound, and 'imitating the Ancients'—Horace and Juvenal in satire, for example—was the natural discipline for all who aspired to literary success, so much so that some founding in the classics is a necessary requisite for a thorough understanding of the literature of the age. There were some who saw that this reliance upon the classics carried its dangers: Cowley, for example, in the Preface to his poems had pointed out that over-dependence could produce works that were nothing more than 'Cold-meats of the Antients, new-heated'. But on the whole most critics would have subscribed to Pope's words, 'Those who say our thoughts are not our own because they resemble the Antients, may as well say our Faces are not our own because they are like our Fathers'.'

The influence of classical criticism was supplemented by that of seventeenth-century France (itself of course influenced by the classical writers). One of the more valuable results of the Civil War had been the close contact between the Royalist exiles and the culture and manners of the court of Louis XIV. There was indeed a considerable cultural interchange between the two countries throughout the Augustan Age (it was by no means a one-way traffic) and this was important because it meant that English literature, for the first time on such a scale, now entered into the European mainstream.

As far as criticism was concerned Boileau's *L'Art Poétique* was revered almost as much as Horace's *Ars Poetica*: there were a number of translations and adaptations, and Pope's *An Essay on Criticism* set out to emulate it. There were translations, too, of Rapin's critical writings and Dryden described Boileau and Rapin as 'the greatest of this age' in the field of critical theory.

The major French influence on Dryden's own criticism was that of Corneille, whose critical introductions to his plays inspired Dryden's Prefaces. Dryden, however, was no slavish imitator, and although Ben Jonson in his critical jottings had to some extent anticipated him, the bulk of pre-Restoration criticism appears archaic and formless beside the civilized, reasonable discourse of such masterpieces as *An Essay of Dramatick Poesie* and the *Preface to*

85

the Fables, Ancient and Modern, and Dryden certainly deserves the title 'the father of English literary criticism'.

This, it is true, was a department of literary activity in which the Augustans revealed some of their most irritating limitations, and Dryden was no exception. He was as reverent a disciple of the Ancients as any of his contemporaries and, as in the cases of Waller and Denham, just as prone to the kind of distorted judgments that inevitably sprang from the complacent and over-confident estimation that regarded English culture of the past as still in the apprenticeship stage and that of the present as the final perfect flowering.

Nevertheless Dryden was far less deferential to 'the Rules' than most of the critics, and time after time his good sense and his good taste triumphed. Though, for example, he could venture to 'modernize' Chaucer and Shakespeare, by eliminating what he regarded as the ignorant barbarities of their styles, he could at the same time pay eloquent tribute to their genius and his critical writings are full of valuable insights.

Much the same can be said of Dr Johnson who is the other really major critic of the age, though a number of other writers, among them Cowley, Swift, Addison, and Sir Joshua Reynolds, had important contributions to make. It has already been pointed out how Johnson in his *Lives of the Most Eminent Poets* in making stringent criticisms of those whose work was alien to his own tastes or to those of the age, nevertheless frequently put his finger on the fundamental truths about them. Although, too, in the Preface to his edition of Shakespeare he blames Shakespeare for neglecting some of the classical 'Rules', and makes a number of criticisms that sound ridiculous to modern readers, he responds deeply to his genius in the portrayal of character. The outstanding features of Johnson's criticism are honesty and humanity. He proceeds from too narrow a basis, but this at least gave him discipline and there is nothing flaccid or wavering in his judgments. Where necessary, too, he can put his prejudices in abeyance: Shakespeare's mixture of tragedy and comedy, for example, was on the whole wrong in principle and in his view *ought* not to have worked, but he acknowledged that usually it did. In Johnson, too, there is always the feeling that behind all the rules and principles lies his actual, living experience and that in the last resort this must be the true touchstone. Though he subscribed whole-heartedly to the critical traditions of his age, he was independent in his interpretation of them: 'Reason wants not Horace to support it', he declared:

86

'There is always an appeal open from criticism to nature', and he had no patience with those who 'draw their principles of judgment rather from books than from reason'.

If the 'proper study of mankind' was man, then criticism of society was even more obligatory than criticism of literature—and the chief instrument of this criticism was satire. To many satire appears as a purely negative approach to life which releases emotions that are disruptive and harmful. This was the reverse of the intention of the Augustans, who scourged the vices and follies of society because they felt they threatened that order and unity they prized so highly. It was an attitude that involved a considerable expenditure of energy upon the ephemeral and the trivial. There were, for example, the long-forgotten objects of Pope's spleen in *The Dunciad*, and there are whole tracts of Augustan satire by writers great and small which are rightly lost to oblivion. But that positive moral and imaginative values can attend satire is also amply demonstrated by the poetry of the period, and above all by that of Pope. Even when he is at his most mocking there are flashes of moral illumination in which the terrors of death and disease are suddenly revealed lurking below the pomp and glitter of the fashionable world. In Epistle II of *The Moral Essays*, for example, there is a terrifying vision of old age as the culmination of a wasted life:

> 'See how the world its veterans rewards!
> A youth of frolics, an old age of cards;
> Fair to no purpose, artful to no end,
> Young without lovers, old without a friend;
> A fop their passion and their prize a sot;
> Alive ridiculous, and dead, forgot!'

Even at his most savage, too, Pope often elevates his target to the stature of an allegorical, almost universal, figure—as with the pitiful Lord Hervey in the *Epistle to Dr Arbuthnot*:

> 'Satire or sense, alas can Sporus feel?
> Who breaks a butterfly upon a wheel?'

Pope was the supreme satirical poet of the age—as he is of English poetry in general—but other poets at times came close to him. Dryden had the same power of universalizing his victims, as with the unforgettable portrait of Shaftesbury in *Absalom and Achitophel*; Rochester's savagery was as intense in *A Satyr Against Mankind*, and

87

a serious moral purpose lies behind it; and there can certainly be no doubting the intention of Johnson's two powerful satires, *London: A Poem in Imitation of the Third Satire of Juvenal* and *The Vanity of Human Wishes*, which was also an imitation of Juvenal. Matthew Prior writes of the fashionable world in an easy witty vernacular, but though he has nothing like the high seriousness of Johnson he too is not without a moral point of view, and even Restoration comedy, though for the most part it portrays a world lacking in principle, sometimes implies a positive standard of reference, particularly in the plays of William Congreve.

The greatest rival to Pope in the field of satire, however, was Jonathan Swift. Swift's genius is so powerful and varied, and so baffling, that any summary of his work is bound to be ridiculously over-simplified. In order to do it justice it would be necessary, for one thing, to examine the astonishing variety of his dialectical methods and the equally astonishing variety of his prose resources which make him not only the culminating-point of that development initiated by Dryden, but also one of the greatest and most complex prose writers in the language.

Swift was also one of the most devastating critics of the contemporary scene. The range of the targets he chose also makes him one of the most comprehensive. They include the absolutist ideas of Hobbes, the controversy between Ancients and Moderns (and the malignity of critics in general), the depredations of the English upon the Irish, the lukewarmness of contemporary Christianity, the cynicism and cruelty of European power politics, and many others. Merely to compile a list is to make a tally of the areas where the age was most vulnerable.

His basic weapon was a kind of grotesque mockery accompanied by an imperturbable air of gravity. It had something in common with Butler's *Hudibras* and Defoe's *The Shortest Way with Dissenters*, and with Rabelais, but Swift's irony is the more subtle and disturbing. His technique is usually a double-edged one. Thus in the most famous of his pamphlets, *A Modest Proposal for Preventing the Children of the Poor from Being a Burthen to their Parents or Country, and for making them Beneficial to the Publick*, he does not directly attack the oppression of the Irish poor by their English landlords, but tongue-in-cheek pretends to be making a sober proposal for the solution of the problem, which turns out to be even more monstrous (no less than the breeding of children for meat)—with the result that the real cruelty is left mercilessly exposed.

Similarly in his pamphlet *Argument to Prove the Inconvenience of*

Abolishing Christianity he adopts an eminently reasonable, button-holing tone which draws the reader unconsciously along with him —only to realize, at the very moment the mat is neatly pulled from under his feet, that he cannot and must not agree: 'I hope no reader imagines me so weak as to stand up in the Defence of Real Christianity, such as used in Primitive Times (if we may believe the Authors of those Ages) to have an Influence upon Mens Belief and Actions: To offer at the restoring of that would indeed be a wild Project...' The drift of the argument here is towards assent, but its content demands rejection, and the pull between the two sets up a continuous and disturbing tension in the reader's mind.

The effect is often complicated because the targets can suddenly disappear and new ones appear in their place. His satire can very well turn against those whose sympathies it is supposed to enlist as well as against those it is designed to expose. The morbid element in Swift's temperament bred a savage disgust that at times extends to the whole of humanity. Even in the early *A Tale of a Tub* this disgust, against the overt trend of the satire, can flash out with sardonic and often sadistic effect as with the ferocious aside: 'Last week I saw a Woman flay'd, and you will hardly believe, how much it alter'd her Person for the worse.' And in the immortal *Travels into Several Remote Nations of the World, by Lemuel Gulliver, first a Surgeon, and then a Captain of Several Ships* his misanthropy finds bitter expression in the words of the King of the Brobdingnags, after Gulliver has given him an account of the affairs of contemporary Europe: '... I cannot but conclude the Bulk of your Nations to be the most pernicious race of little odious Vermin that Nature ever suffered to crawl upon the Surface of the Earth.'

The fact, however, that Swift's satire turned in upon itself to the extent of nullifying its ostensible moral purpose does not detract from the greatness of his work. Like all great works of art, it possesses its own inherent vitality and its own laws of being, derived from the force of its creator's genius and the depths of his own sufferings.

Dr Johnson's novel *The History of Rasselas, Prince of Abyssinia*, like Voltaire's *Candide*, also satirized the self-satisfied optimism of the times. There is mockery, too, in Fielding's novels, but the tone is more good-natured than anything in Swift. And there is certainly nothing of Swift's ferocity in the portraits of Sir Andrew Freeport, Captain Sentry, Will Honeycomb, and the immortal Sir Roger de Coverley in *The Spectator*, where the satire is gentle and corrective in intention.

English Literature

The spirit of satire informs a good deal of the general prose of the period, as witness the ironical tone of some of the passages (and particularly those dealing with Christianity) in Edward Gibbon's *The Decline and Fall of the Roman Empire*. This great work with its solemn and majestic panorama of human power and pride is symptomatic of the enthusiasm for historical writings of all kinds.

The first fruits of this particular enthusiasm had been the Earl of Clarendon's *The True Historical Narrative of the Rebellion and Civil Wars in England* and—written from a Whig standpoint—Gilbert Burnet's *The History of My Own Times*, both of which were published in the first quarter of the eighteenth century, though composed earlier. They are impressive works, but they are transitional in style and approach and (especially in the case of Clarendon) still not so very far removed from the Elizabethan Chronicles. The contrast with Gibbon's sophisticated and scholarly approach is a measure of the tremendous advances achieved by English prose in the intervening years.

An equally sophisticated, if partisan, treatment of semi-historical material marks Swift's longer political pamphlets with their highly efficient marshalling of fact and argument, and the writings of Henry Saint-John, Viscount Bolingbroke, especially in *The Idea of a Patriot King*. History as personally experienced also figures increasingly in the prose of the period. In addition to Defoe's description of his journeys, which are still of great interest to social and economic historians, there were Horace Walpole's memoirs of the reigns of George II and George III, and Arthur Young's account of his travels in France (an important contribution to the understanding of the economic factors behind the French Revolution).

It was inevitable, too, that in an age so devoted to social record there should be a considerable expansion of biographical writing. The supreme achievement in this *genre* was James Boswell's *The Life of Dr Samuel Johnson*, not only an account of his hero's life but one in which his own personality is so strongly asserted that subject and author are inextricably merged. Thanks to some of the most sensational literary discoveries of the present century in the form of Boswell's *Journals*, Boswell himself is now beginning to emerge as one of the most significant writers of the period, and certainly the greatest contributor to our knowledge of the social life of the second half of the eighteenth century.

A summary of Augustan prose would also be incomplete without some mention of the letter writers, and it is significant that letters were often published in collections, as with those of Lady Mary Wortley Montagu, whose vigorous phrase and candid mind relate her to Jane Austen. Other notable letter writers were Horace Walpole, William Cowper, and William Shenstone, while the letters of Thomas Gray contain deeper and more emotional qualities, as well as some outstanding pieces of natural description that point forward to the Romantic Revival.

The perfecting of an easier prose style is reflected too in the steady increase of autobiographical writings, diaries, and journals —but most strikingly of all in the development of the essay form. There could be no greater contrast than that between Bacon's essays with their clipped, antithetical style, and the easy urbane grace which in the hands of Steele, Addison, Goldsmith, and many others turned the essay into an artistic unit, self-contained but without any sense of constriction.

The two dominant literary forms of the age, indeed, were the essay and the novel—and they were closely connected. A number of the essays in the periodicals—and notably some of those by Steele, Addison, and Johnson—are virtually short stories, and the approach of the periodical essayists in their presentation of manners and behaviour is largely fictional. The Spectator Club, for example, with its gallery of contemporary portraits in its original conception aimed at being a kind of eighteenth-century *Canterbury Tales*, and the style and method of the essayists, and even some of their character-types, are frequently in evidence in the novels of the period. But in order to appreciate the way in which the novel finally took precedence and absorbed some of the most vital elements of the age it is also necessary to pay some attention to the place occupied by the drama.

The first point to be noted here is that early on drama lost all effective contact with poetry. Whereas in the sixteenth and seventeenth centuries there were few major poets who were not also dramatists, and vice versa (even Milton wrote *Comus* and *Samson Agonistes*), it was now possible for a poet like Pope to achieve a great reputation without any practical contact with the theatre at all.

When the theatres reopened at the Restoration it is true that some traces of the great tradition lingered on for a while. Ben Jonson, for example, was still popular. Shakespeare's plays were still frequently performed—but (and this is the telling point) usually in the shape of 'adaptations'. Thus *Romeo and Juliet* was given a happy ending, and Dryden added various indecencies to *The Tempest* in order to bring it into line with existing fashions. Even Beaumont and Fletcher's *The Maid's Tragedy* was watered down. The truth of the matter was that the pleasure-seeking court audiences could not stomach anything approaching authentic tragedy.

The only real interest today of the 'heroic' plays of this period lies in the finality with which they demonstrate this fact. The best of them was probably Dryden's *Aurung-Zebe, or the Great Mogul*, which at least contains some effective and colourful rhetoric and a skilful handling of the couplet. But the extravagance and falsity of plot, situation, and characterization, and the stilted declamatory nature of the verse in nearly all of these plays make them pitiful substitutes for the tragedies of the great tradition.

Dryden's *All for Love, or the World Well Lost*, which was written in blank verse and contained plausible characters and situations, was, it is true, in a different category—but a comparison with Shakespeare's *Antony and Cleopatra* is almost entirely to Dryden's disadvantage. And although many other tragedies were written, some original, some translations or adaptations from Corneille and Racine, the only other one throughout the whole period that merits any serious mention was Thomas Otway's *Venice Preserved*, which recaptured something of the fire and vigour of Thomas Kyd's *The Spanish Tragedie*.

Comedy possessed considerably more vitality and staying-power. Most of its characters were shallow, flippant, and immoral, but unlike those of the heroic drama they were taken from life. The dialogue in such plays as Dryden's *The Wild Gallant* or Vanbrugh's *The Relapse* was in consequence sharp, witty, and realistic. Many of these playwrights, too, benefited from the example of Molière across the Channel—as with Wycherley's *The Country Wife*, while *The Plain Dealer* by the same author in addition made good use of the influence of Ben Jonson's London comedies, and even contained echoes of Shakespearian comedy.

There are Shakespearian touches, too, in Congreve's *The Way of the World*, especially in the raillery of Mirabell and Millamant, which has something of the charm and even the tenderness of that of Benedick and Beatrice in *Much Ado About Nothing*. Congreve indeed is the most accomplished of the Restoration writers of comedy, and though his world is no more inspiring than that of his fellows, the very completeness and polish of its portrayal suggest the existence of a serious satirical purpose.

Dr Johnson and Boswell in Edinburgh by Samuel Collings, 1786

A Gillray cartoon, showing Sheridan, dressed as Harlequin, leading the forces of the professionals against the amateurs of the Pic-Nic Society. The actors follow in characteristic attitudes—Kemble as Hamlet, Mrs Billington singing, Mrs Siddons (? as Lady Macbeth). On the stage Lady Buckingham (front), Lady Salisbury (behind in profile), Lord Cholmondeley as King Pic-Nic, 1802

But Restoration comedy like the heroic drama was really valid only in the context of the courtly and fashionable audiences for whom it was designed. Its indecencies were alien to middle-class tastes, which explains the great stir made by Jeremy Collier's *A Short View of the Immorality and Profaneness of the English Stage* (1698) backed by clerical opinion of all denominations.

As a result probably of this expression of public opinion, the comedies of the Irishman George Farquhar contain fewer indecencies, less viciousness of behaviour, and also a certain charm derived from their author's temperament. Even more interesting is the fact that both *The Recruiting Officer* and *The Beaux' Stratagem* mark a break with Restoration tradition by taking the characters out of fashionable drawing-rooms and into country inns, country-houses, the highway, and the open air, and by introducing representatives of the 'lower orders'. Farquhar's plays, therefore, besides anticipating Sheridan are drawing closer to the kind of world portrayed, with so much more scope and variety, in the novels of Henry Fielding.

Middle-class tastes, however, were more deliberately catered for by playwrights such as George Lillo in a new type of domestic drama, which produced little of worth but which contained the seeds of modern social and realistic drama as well as anticipating Victorian melodrama and, surprisingly, exercising an influence upon the plays of Diderot, one of the 'fathers' of the French Revolution. But it was the numerous sentimental comedies of the eighteenth century, such as Richard Steele's *The Tender Husband*, which corresponded most directly of all to middle-class sensibilities. In neither of these developments, however, was there anything that remotely suggested a revival of a national drama.

Towards the end of the eighteenth century, it is true, Oliver Goldsmith rescued drama from the depths into which it had fallen with several excellent plays, notably *She Stoops to Conquer*, the only play of the whole period, apart from those of Sheridan, which retains a regular place in the modern repertoire. Goldsmith's humane temperament shines through this fine comedy and his characters have a freshness and reality which had been lacking for years: Mr and Mrs Hardcastle, for example, might have come from a novel by Jane Austen.

It is Richard Brinsley Sheridan, however, who represents the last sunset glow of a great tradition. Like Goldsmith he attacked the sentimentalists, as in his portrait of Lydia Languish in *The Rivals*, a play which recaptures the vigorous comic invention and the sparkling wit of Vanbrugh and Congreve. As for *The School for Scandal*, this was probably the greatest achievement in English comedy since Shakespeare—and the juxtaposition of the brothers Charles and Joseph Surface interestingly recalls that of Orlando and Oliver in *As You Like It*. Its satire of scandal-mongering and hypocrisy, moreover, has something of the force of the old Moralities and of Ben Jonson's comedy. Jonson's influence, indeed, is apparent, both in this play and in *The Critic*, a genuine satire of human folly with a real concern for literary, social, and moral values.

Goldsmith and Sheridan, however, are exceptions to the general rule: they had no successors and English drama in the last decades of the eighteenth century rapidly degenerated. It was symptomatic of the final decline, as well as of the fact that fiction had largely absorbed the energies which once went into a national drama, that the theatre was increasingly driven to rely upon stage adaptations of novels.

This does not mean that at the level of simple entertainment the drama was not popular. On the contrary, it was an age of ardent theatre-going, during which many famous theatres were built. It was also an age of great actresses and actors, but the fact that the names of Woffington, Siddons, Macklin, Kemble, and Garrick survive while the plays in which they acted are for the most part forgotten is yet further evidence that the drama of the age was a predominantly *social* activity rather than an important organization of its profoundest imaginative energies.

The main conditions for the rise of the novel were therefore present by about 1740. A firm and supple prose-style was to hand, while the vacuum created by the decline of the drama was waiting to be filled. In particular there was the large potential public of the middle classes who, still influenced by Puritan ideas, distrusted the theatre but, better educated than they had been in the past and in an age of comparative peace and prosperity with far more leisure, were ready for a form of entertainment that would fill it without any danger of moral impropriety.

The periodicals only partially satisfied the middle-class appetite, and women readers in particular wanted something more emotionally stimulating. Translations of French romances had long been popular, and there had been a few English competitors such as Aphra Behn's *Oroonoko; or the History of the Royal Slave*, whose hero foreshadowed the 'Noble Savage' of the Romantics. There were of course Defoe's realistic novels, but popular though they were they contained little sense of human character and its development, while Bunyan's *The Pilgrim's Progress* and Swift's *Gulliver's Travels*, in spite of their brilliant narrative qualities, were only indirectly novels. What was lacking was a contemporary Chaucer of fiction, someone who could create characters in the round with independent emotional existences who were not primarily puppets manipulated in the service of a religious or political idea.

The great historical importance of Samuel Richardson is that he fulfilled so many of these conditions. He belonged to the middle classes and was Puritan by inclination. From an early age he had been a kind of father-confessor to the women of his acquaintance, and the feminine component in his own make-up was highly developed. The genesis of his first novel *Pamela; or Virtue Rewarded* (1740–1) was characteristic: it was a project for a series of letters which would serve as models for 'handsome girls' in domestic service, with guidance on how to avoid 'the snares that might be laid against their virtue'.

The defects in this and Richardson's subsequent novels make a formidable tally. The clumsy epistolary device was used in all of them and involved intolerable prolixity—including in Pamela's case the improbability that she could have had either the education or the leisure to write at such length. They are often pompous and tedious, and they are completely lacking in humour. They are relentlessly didactic, and yet in many respects they are morally repulsive: Pamela's virtue, for example, emerges merely as a commodity to be cunningly bargained for; Lovelace in *Clarissa Harlowe; or The History of a Young Lady* is a brutal ravisher with hardly a redeeming feature; and the hero of *The History of Sir Charles Grandison* is a pompous prig. There is moreover something distinctly morbid about Richardson's preoccupation with the protection of female sexual virtue. Yet in spite of these faults Richardson's novels are important landmarks in the history of the English novel, and not only because of their tremendous contemporary popularity and their great influence on the Continent.

For one thing, each of them constitutes a genuine world of the imagination, controlled by a single and unified vision. When once the conventions governing that world have been accepted, his characters emerge as real and three-dimensional. Their actions become convincing when related to that world, and their emotions genuine and moving. Even the prolixity reveals merits of suspense. This is particularly the case in *Clarissa Harlowe* where the heroine's

95

long-drawn-out agony manages to retain genuine intensity without losing the sense of tragic inevitability. It is in this novel, in fact, that the spirit of tragedy which had long since abandoned the drama must be sought.

Richardson's most distinctive quality is undoubtedly his psychological penetration. It is not only that he conducts a subtle and minute scrutiny of his characters' feelings, but also that, at a subconscious level, he deals with motivations that are intrinsic to human relationships, between parents and children as well as between the sexes: this helps to explain the revulsion which his characters frequently inspire—but it also helps to explain their hypnotic appeal.

It was Richardson, therefore, who raised the English novel to the status of a serious art-form, which it had already attained on the Continent in the hands of such great writers as Cervantes. At the same time he was responsible not only for initiating the psychological novel, which culminated in such great twentieth-century practitioners as Henry James, Joseph Conrad, and D. H. Lawrence, but indirectly the opposite kind that eventually reached its peak in Charles Dickens.

For it was as a parody of *Pamela* that Henry Fielding wrote *The History of the Adventures of Joseph Andrews and his Friend Mr Abraham Adams*, in which Pamela's imagined brother is called upon to defend *his* virtue against the wiles of his employer Lady Booby, and which launched Fielding upon his career as a great novelist.

Fielding's novels are straightforward picaresque adventure stories, but though he does not have Richardson's letter-writing device to handicap him, his work, from the point of view of the art of fiction, is in many respects more defective and primitive. He continually intrudes himself in the action, for example, commenting, exhorting, declaiming, and acting as garrulous puppet-master. The opening chapters of several of the books of *Joseph Andrews* and of all of them in *The History of Tom Jones, A Foundling* are literary essays such as might have appeared in one of the periodicals, and are completely detachable.

Fielding's novels in fact do not mark such a revolutionary departure as Richardson's. They derive directly from the mock-heroic tradition (in which a sardonic commentator preserving a separate identity is one of the conventions) and are close in manner to other mock-heroic works of the period, and are often strikingly similar in tone and approach to Swift. The old Morality tradition, by way of Ben Jonson, also survives in them and the names of many of the characters—Mr Allworthy in *Tom Jones*, for example—are semi-allegorical. The influence of the Elizabethan picaresque writers, especially that of Nashe, is also evident.

Fielding's novels can also be related to the medieval tradition of satire on human folly and to the work of Rabelais and Cervantes. Parson Adams in *Joseph Andrews*, for example, often invites comparison with Don Quixote, and the schoolmaster Partridge who accompanies Tom Jones on his travels has something in common with Sancho Panza.

But Fielding's genius transformed the conventions in which he worked. His mock-heroic, for example, is attended by an astonishing fertility of comic invention that recalls Shakespeare and Chaucer. Mrs Slipslop, Mrs Tow-wouse, and Parson Trulliber in *Joseph Andrews* are among the great comic characters of English literature, and Molly Seagrim's mock-Homeric battle in the churchyard—in *Tom Jones*—is among its greatest comic passages.

His novels are 'novels of manners', but with the possible exception of some of the virtuous characters, like Mr Allworthy in *Tom Jones* and Amelia in the novel of that name, his characters are not types but human beings endowed with abundant life of their own. He certainly has a satirical purpose, which in *Amelia*—probably as a result of his experiences as a magistrate—is sometimes intrusive though it also has a Hogarth-like particularity. He is also very careful to stress the religious assumptions of the age, but his approach to them represents the practical Christianity of the Augustans at its best.

It is Fielding's firm but genial humanity that is his greatest asset. He can depict goodness, as in Parson Adams, but he can also see the goodness in ordinary weak mortals. To him the most valuable human qualities are courage, frankness, and generosity. Because Tom Jones possesses these his creator can readily forgive him his sins of the flesh. Where men act from impulse, he implies, they are alive and their hearts are open: it is action proceeding from calculation that he distrusts, and selfishness and hypocrisy are the sins he most condemns.

Gifts such as Fielding possessed might in another age have qualified him for the role of great dramatist. He did indeed write a great deal for the theatre, and it was the satirical daring of one of his plays that was in large part responsible for the Licensing Act of 1737 which further emasculated the drama. It was a sound instinct, however, and a lucky one for English literature, that prompted him to abandon the theatre for a form better suited to the imaginative energies of the age.

Richardson and Fielding of course had their predecessors, as earlier chapters have indicated. But it was they who set English fiction on its path to greatness, and within little more than thirty years of the appearance of *Pamela* the tradition of the English novel of character, action, and humour was to all intents and purposes fully formed. In addition Richardson and Fielding represent the two basic modes of fiction—of which Dostoevsky and Tolstoy were to be the supreme examples—that of psychological drama on the one hand, and that of epic spaciousness on the other.

The stature of Tobias Smollett and Laurence Sterne is not commensurate with that of Richardson and Fielding and their novels do not form such coherent wholes. Smollett's are for the most part episodic, often drawing in documentary detail upon his personal experiences, especially in *Roderick Random* (1748). His last novel, *The Expedition of Humphry Clinker*, published twenty years later, followed Richardson's epistolary technique, but has little plot or development of character. On the other hand, the sea setting of *Roderick Random* and *Peregrine Pickle* further extended the scope of fiction, and Smollett's ferocious realism in them generates its own moral comment; *Humphry Clinker* is more humane in approach and presents a valuable picture of the various forces at work towards the close of the Augustan era, including those of 'sensibility' and Methodism which both looked forward to certain aspects of the Romantic Revival.

Sterne's *The Life and Opinions of Tristram Shandy, Gentleman* has been described as 'mainly a vast digression', while *A Sentimental Journey through France and Italy* is also a rambling piece of fiction rather than a novel in any artistic sense of the term. Sterne's frame of mind and compendious approach are similar to those of earlier eccentrics such as Burton and Browne, and he is also indebted to Rabelais and Cervantes. But in spite of archaic elements and defective structure these novels are important works of fiction, and Sterne's verbal and stylistic acrobatics (though attended by a good deal of prurience) are often extremely funny besides containing the germs of later developments, including the novels built upon the 'free association of ideas' or 'the flow of consciousness'.

The period produced other novels which are either of intrinsic merit—such as Goldsmith's mellow and humane comedy *The Vicar of Wakefield* and Fanny Burney's sprightly *Evelina* with its foretaste of Jane Austen—or interesting as symptoms of new tendencies—as with Henry Mackenzie's *The Man of Feeling* and Horace Walpole's *The Castle of Otranto*. But it was Richardson, Fielding, Smollett, and Sterne who between them erected the most impressive monument to the vitality and variety of the Augustan Age.

Descriptive labels such as 'Classical', 'Augustan', 'The Age of Reason' and 'The Age of Prose' can be applied to this period more confidently than to most, because the prevailing preoccupation with social order and balance gave it unusual coherence. Nothing would be farther from the truth, however, than to suppose that strong feeling did not exist. It is instructive to note, for example, that the most influential work of classical criticism next to that of Horace was Longinus' treatise *On the Sublime*, which praises passion and ecstasy. The feeling was there—but the whole point is that it was kept under strict control in deference to an ideal of civilized behaviour that was itself strongly felt.

The suspicion that this control might be too rigorously applied was, moreover, present throughout the period. As early as 1711, for example, the Earl of Shaftesbury (grandson of Dryden's 'Achitophel') in his philosophical work *Characteristicks of Men, Manners, Opinions, Times* was stressing the importance of 'our passions and affections', and a year later Addison was writing a whole series in *The Spectator* upon 'The Pleasures of Imagination'. By about the middle of the eighteenth century the brothers Joseph and Thomas Warton and others were beginning to criticize Pope and his kind of poetry on the grounds that it lacked the 'nobler' qualities of the earlier English poets.

There were doubts about the prevailing temper of poetry among the poets themselves. As early as 1726 James Thomson was demanding that poetry should be rescued from social satire by a return to 'great and serious subjects' such as occur in 'wild and romantic country', and in *The Seasons*, though the language and imagery are fundamentally Augustan, he tried to put his precepts into practice. A number of other poets, among them William Shenstone, Edward Dyer, Mark Akenside, William Cowper, and William Collins, also reacted to natural scenery with at least some approximation to the freshness of Wordsworth and the Lake poets. The Romantic emotion of melancholy figured in Edward Young's *The Complaint, or Night Thoughts on Life, Death and Immortality*, and the Romantic preoccupation with the Middle Ages and with Norse mythology was anticipated in some of the shorter poems of

Thomas Gray. William Collins's *Popular Superstitions of the Highlands* anticipates another of the Romantic enthusiasms—and there were at least three thorough-going precursors of the Romantic Revival in James Macpherson, Thomas Percy, and Thomas Chatterton.

The poems which Macpherson attributed to a mythical Celtic bard whom he called Ossian were mainly his own, but they fed a growing appetite for ancient themes and backgrounds and wielded an enormous influence. They probably led the youthful Chatterton to try his own hand at literary forgery in the poems which he claimed to have been written by an imaginary fifteenth-century monk named Rowley, but which nevertheless contain the genuine Romantic aura, while the tragic circumstances of his early death in 1770 make him the very prototype of the 'Romantic poet'. And finally Percy's collection of genuine old ballads and other poems in *Reliques of Ancient English Poetry* sounded a music very different from that of the heroic couplet and was in the direct line of descent to Coleridge's *The Ancient Mariner*.

Other anticipations of Romanticism—and notably the cult of sensibility, issuing, especially after the middle of the eighteenth century, in practical humanitarianism, and the Methodist Movement (which began about 1738)—have already been indicated and there were many more. In other words, Classicism itself contained the seeds of Romanticism, and one is tempted to add that the reverse was also true—for these two terms refer not only to periods of literary history but also to two complementary faculties of the human mind.

Frontispiece Vol.1.

W.Hogarth inv.t   Vol.2.page 128.   S.Ravenet Sculp.t

Illustration by Hogarth for *Tristram Shandy* by Laurence Sterne, 1760

Chatterton taking a bowl of poison by John Flaxman

5 · The Romantic Revival

I F English literature from the Restoration to the beginning of the French Revolution (to choose two arbitrary limits) can be described as an 'age of prose', then there is no doubt that the period that followed it can be called 'the age of poetry'. Its greatest achievements were in this field, and though the writers of the period were at variance in many respects—including their estimation of the Augustan style of writing—they were at one in their belief in the pre-eminence of poetry.

It would indeed not be far from the mark to substitute for the term 'Romantic Revival' that of 'revival of poetry', for it was just those modes of feeling that find their natural outlet in poetry which now came breaking through the artificial barriers imposed by the Augustans. Whereas they had believed that the emotions should be kept under control in the service of social propriety, the emphasis now was on their liberation: as William Wordsworth declared in his Preface to the *Lyrical Ballads*, 'all good poetry is the spontaneous overflow of powerful feelings'.

The whole conception of poetry, therefore, changed out of all recognition. 'Its object', Wordsworth argued, 'is truth not individual and local, but general and operative; not standing upon external testimony, but carried alive into the heart by passion.' This is very far from Pope's social view of poetry as expressed in his Preface to *An Essay on Man*—and in his own verse—and so is Wordsworth's belief in poetry not merely as the servant of man's rational and social investigations but as something above them, something that in itself partakes of religion and philosophy: 'Poetry is the breath and finer spirit of all knowledge; it is the impassioned expression which is the countenance of all Science.'

Even more sweeping claims for the superiority of poetry over the kinds of knowledge represented by science was made by Percy Bysshe Shelley in *A Defence of Poetry* (1821): 'Poetry is indeed something divine. It is at once the centre and circumference of knowledge; it is that which comprehends all science, and that to which all science must be referred.'

What, too, would Pope and his contemporaries have made of

Shelley's belief that poetry arrested 'the vanishing apparitions which haunt the interlunations of life', and that it redeemed 'from decay the visitations of the divinity in man'? These were ideas never dreamed of in their philosophy, and the language in which they were expressed would probably have struck them as amorphous and meaningless. But the poet is no longer content to aim merely at 'what oft was thought but ne'er so well expressed'. His function now is to illuminate, to reveal, to lead forward to new spiritual experiences, not just to observe and record. Out of the phenomena presented to him he claims to create a new dimension: or as Shelley put it in *Prometheus Unbound*:

> 'Forms more real than living man,
> Nurslings of immortality.'

The familiar is therefore no longer the touchstone: on the contrary, Shelley says, the poet 'strips the veil of familiarity from the world, and lays bare the naked and sleeping beauty, which is the spirit of its forms'. His circuit is no longer that of a compact and well-organized society existing in a finite time and place: it is, Wordsworth declares, 'the vast empire of human society, as it is spread over the whole earth, and over all time' which the poet must bind together 'by passion and knowledge'. Indeed the poet, according to these new interpretations, is not necessarily interested in society, as Pope understood the term, or even *in* it. He is, Shelley suggests, 'a nightingale, who sits in darkness and sings to cheer its own solitude with sweet sounds'. His contemplation can be entirely inward—as so often with William Blake—and if, like Byron or like Shelley, he is an enemy of organized society his relevance is in no way impaired. For the Romantic conception of the poet places him above society, as the seer or prophet, or as Shelley proudly acclaims, 'the unacknowledged legislator of the world'.

When, therefore, Keats in one of his letters says 'I am convinced more and more that fine writing is next to fine doing, the top thing in the world' he is certainly not echoing Pope's call to verbal exactitude, for if the poet is to be considered as a prophet or *vates*, then he is subject to divine visitations and the 'word' will express itself through him as well as be expressed *by* him. To some extent he will be a mouth-piece, or rather an oracle, through whom the 'voice of the god' may speak with mysterious and awe-inspiring effect.

With poetry of this kind there was no question of formulating the meaning or calculating the effects in advance: for the Romantics the language of poetry was not, as it had been for Pope, a matter of finalizing an experience like a butterfly transfixed by a pin, but of letting the shaping powers of the imagination take control, of submitting it to largely unconscious processes. 'Language', Shelley says, 'is arbitrarily produced by the imagination, and has no relation to thoughts alone' and in his view poets are 'the hierophants of an unapprehended inspiration' who deal with 'words which express what they understand not'.

This was admittedly one of the extreme views and would not have been accepted by all Shelley's contemporaries, but it represents an extremely important aspect of Romanticism. There were occasions when it led to woolliness and imprecision, but it was also responsible for some of the most subtle and beautiful poetry in the English language—poetry in which the reader feels that the poet is trusting his language, letting it carry him as the imagination dictates, and achieving new and unexpected effects including at times that 'sense of wonder' which is one of the most exciting characteristics of Romantic poetry.

It was the desire to free language for tasks such as these that caused Wordsworth and Samuel Taylor Coleridge to collaborate in the *Lyrical Ballads* of 1798—an important date in the history of English literature and—in so far as chronology is applicable in such matters—one that can be counted as the real starting-point of the Romantic Revival in English poetry, for Blake's example had come too early, and for most of his contemporaries he remained an eccentric and isolated phenomenon.

Wordsworth's aim in this venture was 'to choose incidents and situations from common life, and to relate or describe them . . . as far as was possible in a selection of language really used by men, and, at the same time, to throw over them a certain colouring of imagination, whereby ordinary things should be presented to the mind in an unusual aspect. . .' Coleridge was to reverse the process by injecting into romantic or supernatural themes a human or 'realistic' interest, 'a semblance of truth sufficient to procure for these shadows of imagination that willing suspension of disbelief for the moment, which constitutes poetic faith'.

Wordsworth's share in the experiment must to some extent be accounted a failure. It is true that the kind of 'real language' he had in mind was one of 'men in a state of vivid sensation', purged of obvious irregularities and vulgarities and fitted to 'metrical arrangement', but he was too intent on proving his theory, and most of his contributions to the *Lyrical Ballads* were marred by a false and often ludicrous simplicity as in such lines as:

> 'And often after sunset, sir,
> When it is light and fair,
> I take my little porringer,
> And eat my supper there.'

In practice, moreover, there was little of 'the language of conversation in the . . . lower classes of society' in these poems and (in spite of his disclaimer) eighteenth-century poetic diction was still present in such terms as 'verdant herb', 'vernal showers', 'balmy night', 'May's dewy prime', and 'the equinoctial deep'.

Nevertheless Wordsworth's theories were of tremendous influence in the revolt against the 'gaudiness and inane phraseology' of the Augustan decline and against the approach symbolized by Gray's dictum that poetry 'has a language peculiar to itself'.

His partial failure in the *Lyrical Ballads* was chiefly because he was not the kind of poet he was pretending to be. Essentially—as Coleridge pointed out in *Biographia Literaria*—he was a 'philosophical' poet. Not indeed in the intellectual or academic sense of the word. Wordsworth had philosophical ideas it is true—in connexion with 'associationism', for example—but his genius lay above all in his ability to carry ideas beyond their intellectual connotations, to submit them to the processes of creative digestion, and to reproduce them in a purely poetic medium that can convey some of the most subtle and valuable aspects of human experience:

> '. . . sensations sweet,
> Felt in the blood and felt along the heart.'

Although, however, in his most important poetry Wordsworth used a subtle and highly charged language very different from that of the uneducated peasant, whether in 'a state of vivid sensation' or not, the subjects of his poetic contemplation *were* to a large extent taken from 'humble and rustic life' in close touch with 'the beautiful and permanent forms of nature'. Part of the greatness of Wordsworth's genius lies in his ability to stimulate the reader's imagination to a pitch of perceptiveness in which he can see a poor beggar, or a leech gatherer, or a field of daffodils, with freshness and wonder, as if they had been newly created.

Coleridge's share in the *Lyrical Ballads* was no less momentous. He contributed only three poems to Wordsworth's twenty—but one of these was *The Rime of the Ancyent Marinere*. There was certainly no question of failure in this case. The 'excellence' which Coleridge aimed at in his handling of the supernatural—to interest 'the affections by the dramatic truth of such emotions as would naturally accompany such situations, supposing them real'—was triumphantly achieved. The greatness of the poem lies above all in its creation of an utterly convincing atmosphere, in which all the events, natural and supernatural, are indeed 'real' and the simplest human emotions combine naturally with the most complex and profound.

The Ancient Mariner was a landmark in English Romanticism because it explored areas of experience which had been neglected for many years, and with an intensity of insight and effect unequalled since Shakespeare's *Macbeth* (with whom the Ancient Mariner has something in common). It is significant, moreover, that in revising the poem Coleridge eliminated many of the more bookishly archaic expressions and rewrote lines in a way which increased their mysterious and evocative power—that is, he made them more 'precise', not as Pope would have understood the word, but as it best served the purposes of the Romantic vision.

With the publication of the *Lyrical Ballads* the tyranny of the heroic couplet was largely broken (though poets such as George Crabbe and Samuel Rogers continued to use it), and the next thirty to forty years witnessed a freedom of verse experimentation, unequalled since the Elizabethans. There was also a remarkable revival of older verse-forms, and although in some cases this led to unfortunate results—as with Keats's attempt to imitate Miltonic blank verse in his *Hyperion*—in many others the Romantic inspiration breathed new life into the old moulds. The ballad of course was one of the most obvious examples, but there was also the revival of the sonnet, reaching its climax in such masterpieces as Wordsworth's *Composed upon Westminster Bridge* (in the 'Shakespearian' mode) and Keats's *On first looking into Chapman's Homer* (in the 'Petrarchan' mode). There was the equally remarkable transformation of the ode, both in its more formal Pindaric shape, as with Wordsworth's *Ode on Intimations of Immortality from Recollections of Early Childhood*, and in free and astonishingly resourceful adaptations such as Shelley's *Ode to the West Wind*, Coleridge's *Dejection, an Ode*, and the odes of Keats, which perhaps represent the peak of the Romantics' achievement in poetry. The Spenserian stanza, which in the Augustan period had lent itself only to frigid imitations, took on fresh and vibrant qualities in Shelley's *Adonais*, inspired by the death of Keats in 1821, and an unexpected dexterity and forcefulness in Byron's *Childe Harold*. Italian verse-forms, too, were brilliantly adapted as with Byron's blending of the *ottava rima* and the English ten-syllable line in his greatest poem, *Don Juan*, and with Shelley's dramatic use of the *terza rima* in *Ode to the West Wind*. Blank verse also revealed new resources, especially in Wordsworth's great autobiographical poems, in Shelley's *Prometheus Unbound*, and in Keats's revision of his Miltonic experiment, *The Fall of Hyperion*. There was the great expansion of narrative poetry, particularly by Byron, Robert Southey, Sir Walter Scott, and Thomas Moore. And there was a general bursting forth of lyrical inspiration, including Shelley's 'liquid music in the word' as the twentieth-century poet Robert Bridges described it.

The very profusion of poetry, however, contained warning signs. Poets, critics, and public alike tended to take it too much for granted. The Romantic poets wrote too much and even the best of them were guilty of serious lapses. In point of bulk Wordsworth's dull and uninspired verse far outweighs the great poetry. Coleridge's output was even more erratic. Shelley was frequently vapid, Keats lush, and Byron vulgarly rhetorical. In this respect the Elizabethans and Jacobeans who wrote less and more consistently were undoubtedly the superiors of the Romantics. At the same time, it was too easy for minor writers to achieve inflated reputations: thus Leigh Hunt was revered in his circle beyond his deserts, Moore's lyrical facility received more than its due, and Francis Jeffrey was able to write of the almost forgotten Felicia Hemans in the august *Edinburgh Review*: 'If taste and elegance . . . be titles to enduring fame, we might venture securely to promise that rich boon to the author before us.' In other words, in the Romantic profusion of feeling and invention was inherent the danger of a lowering of standards—and this was to become increasingly apparent as it passed into its Victorian phase.

In this connexion it is important to emphasize again that Wordsworth's call for a return to the 'language really used by men' was fundamentally a theoretical one. He did not practise it himself, and neither did the other Romantic poets. Byron in *Don Juan* came the closest to the rhythms of conversation, though the deceptively free-and-easy versification is the result of a highly sophisticated art and is highly coloured by his own personal tone. For the most part, however, the Romantics, though they relied upon the rhythms of everyday speech more than the Augustans had done, did so far less than 'Metaphysical' poets such as Donne —and less, of course, than the Elizabethan and Jacobean dramatic poets. A great deal of Romantic poetry in fact was 'literary' in the sense that it was very conscious of its literary heritage, and that it was composed in what Keats called 'an artist's humour'. This did not matter when the poet was in command of his material and fully possessed by his experience, but as the genuine Romantic inspiration waned these tendencies became increasingly apparent, until a type of diction emerged every bit as otiose and artificial as that against which Wordsworth and Coleridge had campaigned. At the same time, the conception of the poet as a prophet or seer persisted even when he no longer had anything to prophesy and even when his visions had fled, so that as the nineteenth century progressed the poet became increasingly remote from the real issues of the day and from the lives of the majority of his fellow-men, retreating further and further into the Romantic Ivory Tower. It was these circumstances that help to explain why in the first two decades of the twentieth century poets reacted so vigorously against the 'Romantic' idea and practice of poetry and turned back beyond both the Victorians and the Romantics to Donne and the 'Metaphysicals'—and even to Pope and Dryden.

One thing that cannot be said of the pre-Victorian Romantic poets, however, is that they showed any wish to retreat from the realities of the day. On the contrary, the majority of them were acutely aware of them. The political events of the period indeed were of such a cataclysmic nature that they could hardly be evaded. The French Revolution in particular dealt such a shattering blow to the Augustan concept of balance and the social order that the kind of writing that was its natural corollary would have been no longer valid or practicable whether Wordsworth and Coleridge had written the *Lyrical Ballads* or not.

Towards the end of the Augustan period the English political system, like poetic diction, had shown ominous signs of hardening, and the French Revolution in consequence had many active sympathizers. Revolutionary clubs were common among artisans and intellectuals alike, and the feelings of most of the ardent young spirits of the day were summed up in Wordsworth's famous lines from *The Prelude*:

> 'Bliss was it in that dawn to be alive,
> But to be young was very heaven!'

For the first generation of Romantic writers indeed the French Revolution was one of the most important traumatic experiences of their lives, and it had a tremendous effect upon their work. In

Blake's case, for instance, it inspired his poem on the subject and his revolutionary fervour combined with the apocalyptic teachings of Swedenborg to produce some of the most thrilling moments in his *Prophetic Books*—as well as some of the most obscure.

As far as Wordsworth was concerned, disillusionment with the Revolution was even more important in its consequences than enthusiasm. It had the effect of making him retreat, not indeed to an Ivory Tower, but away from external events ('the moving accident is not my trade') to the deeper levels of his experience and to an even closer communion with Nature—though in this respect the impact of his relationship with Annette Vallon must also be taken into account. Later on, as the Terror passed into the Napoleonic dictatorship, disillusionment deepened until Wordsworth became (like Coleridge) one of the voices of reaction, and eventually—with disastrous effects for his poetry—a pillar of Victorian respectability and conservatism.

In the realm of ideas politics were of tremendous importance. It is true that the Evangelical Revival led (though in quite different directions) by the Wesley brothers and by George White-field was one of the most powerful of the forces leading to the break-up of eighteenth-century religious formalism and complacency. The influence of German philosophy, particularly of Kant and Schelling, upon this process must not be under-estimated either. Its main interpreter was Coleridge who based his philosophical system upon the Kantian distinction between pure reason and practical reason—in order to trace the limits of the Understanding and to assert the claims of that higher Reason (which did not come into the Augustan philosophical reckoning) which he describes as intuition, spiritual vision, or poesy. Nevertheless to a considerable extent it was political philosophy, at any rate up to the turn of the century, that replaced the rationalistic philosophies of the preceding age.

It was of course Jean Jacques Rousseau—that 'very bad man', according to Dr Johnson—who more than any other of the French *philosophes* seemed to speak for contemporary political and social dissatisfactions of the age, as well as for its emotional and aesthetic sensibilities and its humanitarian aspirations. The opening words of Rousseau's treatise on 'the Social Contract' (1762)—'Man is born free, and everywhere he is in chains'—was a trumpet-blast for English as well as for French intellectuals. Some of the pronouncements in *Émile* had an even greater impact—and notably the first sentence: 'God made all things good; man meddles with

William Wordsworth in old age, by Benjamin Haydon

Hall's library at Margate

them and they become evil.' This concept was one which had a particularly strong appeal for the Romantics. It found expression, for example, in a number of novels of which the best known is *Frankenstein; or, the Modern Prometheus* (1818), written by William Godwin's daughter Mary (who was also Shelley's wife). *Frankenstein* was both a 'horror' novel and a pioneer of modern science-fiction: its man-made monster, with his yearning for love and goodness, has much in common with Rousseau's 'Noble Savage', who is naturally good until corrupted by civilized man.

Shelley himself responded enthusiastically to the idealistic and anarchistic ideas of his father-in-law as expounded in *An Enquiry Concerning Political Justice* (1793), which was one of the most influential books of the period. Under its influence Shelley wrote a number of atheistic and anti-government pamphlets, several of his early poems, including *Queen Mab*, which openly avowed his atheism, and in 1818 *The Revolt of Islam*, which was designed, Shelley declared, to kindle 'within the bosoms of my readers a virtuous enthusiasm for those doctrines of liberty and justice, that faith and hope in something good, which neither violence nor misrepresentation nor prejudice can ever totally extinguish among mankind'. This belief in the 'perfectibility of man' underlies not only Shelley's overtly propagandist poems but many others, including *Prometheus Unbound*, and it was one of the major motifs of the period.

The impact of the rebellion of the American colonists had in many respects been as powerful as that of the French Revolution. Many Englishmen welcomed the revolt because they saw in it a check to the autocratic ambitions of George III, already challenged by politicians such as Charles James Fox and John Wilkes. Many pamphlets were written in support of the American rebels, particularly by Thomas Paine.

The Declaration of American Independence in 1776 and the new democratic American Constitution found a particularly ready response among the English middle classes, who had become increasingly aware of the continued pressure of feudal attitudes and privileges upon their own ambitions. It is important to note that it was from these classes that the majority of the writers of the period were recruited. Although the patronage of the great was still by no means a negligible factor, because of the great expansion of the reading public and the speeding up of publishing and printing processes, the writer was nothing like as dependent on it as he had been in the Augustan Age. The cultural centres were no longer confined to the houses of the great, and it was the *salons* of men of middle-class origin such as William Godwin, Samuel Rogers, Leigh Hunt, John Murray, and Charles Lamb which were the most influential.

The Terror in France and the rise of Napoleon came as a shock to many others besides Wordsworth, though Napoleon had his English admirers, some of whom—including William Hazlitt who wrote a life of his hero—remained faithful even after the outbreak of hostilities between England and France. What was inescapable was that the events leading up to the Battle of Waterloo were as tremendous in their own way as the American and French Revolutions, and they too could hardly fail to leave their impress upon the writers who lived through them.

Jane Austen, it is true, has been criticized on the grounds that she was too remote from these happenings, but her aloofness has been exaggerated. Her novels do in fact give to public and world events the degree of prominence they would naturally assume among the kind of people in the kind of provincial settings she is portraying. To take an obvious example, the Napoleonic Wars in *Pride and Prejudice* mean training-camps and handsome young officers—which is exactly what they *would* mean to Mr Bennett's more flighty daughters: and the effects of war upon the careers of naval officers and upon their social and romantic relationships surely receive a good deal of prominence, both in *Mansfield Park* and *Persuasion*.

All those who were disillusioned, moreover, did not follow Wordsworth and Coleridge into conservatism. Even after Waterloo there were causes to arouse strong emotions among the young and the liberal minded. There was, for example, the campaign against the Prince Regent; there was the reactionary 'Holy Alliance' of the European Powers against which Byron inveighed (at the same time scoffing at the reactionary Lake poets); there were the causes of Italian and Greek independence, with which Byron's name is so gloriously associated; there were the challenges of Parliamentary Reform, Catholic Emancipation, the abolition of slavery in the Colonies, and many others.

But though political events made the greatest stir it is likely that social and economic developments affected the attitudes of the Romantic writers at a far deeper level. The tempo of change had not reached the giddy rate it was to achieve in the latter half of the nineteenth century, but even before the end of the eighteenth it had assumed sufficiently sobering proportions. The most important developments in terms of human adaptation and suffering were the introduction of new techniques and machines in the textiles industries and the speeding up of the enclosure of the common lands. The first of these dealt a shattering blow at the old 'cottage economy', depriving the country-dwellers of the supplementary earnings derived from spinning, weaving, or knitting in their own homes which had kept their living-standards at a bearable level. The second robbed them of grazing for their few animals and of their main source of fuel. The main consequence was the growing depopulation of the countryside and the rapid expansion of the towns. There was no corresponding expansion of amenities, and the manufacturing towns rapidly became places of overcrowding, squalor, and ugliness. The word 'town' therefore no longer stood for a centre of civilized social organization as it had for the Augustans.

Within a few years in fact England had changed into a new type of industrial-capitalist State, and although the worst horrors of the Industrial Revolution were yet to come, there were few who liked the change. This holds good of practically all the Romantic writers, whatever their political alignment—of the Tory Southey as much as of the revolutionary Shelley. All were acutely aware that old values were fast disappearing and that new elements were entering the national life to its detriment. These changes and the problems they raised were of course directly reflected in the many economic and sociological writings of the period—such as those by Jeremy Bentham (the father of Utilitarianism), James Mill, his chief disciple, and the famous—and ominous—*Essay on Population* (1798) by James Malthus. But in one way or another the kind of emotions expressed in Blake's *Holy Thursday* affected most of the Romantic poets:

'Is this a holy thing to see
In a rich and fruitful land,
Babes reduced to misery,
Fed with a cold and usurous hand?'

It was the threat of the new industrialism that goes a long way to explaining the tremendous redeeming and healing power that nature had for the Romantics. In Wordsworth's case indeed there is a very marked reluctance to deal with town life at all. In his narrative poem *Michael*, for example, the young man Luke is quickly dismissed as soon as he leaves the countryside for 'the dissolute city'. But though there were so many factors that *might*

III

have made Wordsworth's absorption in nature escapist, there were others sufficiently powerful to offset them. Chief among these was the seriousness of his moral purpose. He was not concerned with the beauties of nature from a merely aesthetic point of view (as were so many later nature poets), but from the point of view of a whole way of life and a whole range of human values. He was being absolutely sincere when in his Prefaces he declared his belief that people living close to nature were morally in a more healthy condition than those living in towns. For Wordsworth nature was the greatest of all educating and civilizing agencies:

> 'One impulse from a vernal wood
> May teach you more of man,
> Of moral evil and of good,
> Than all the sages can.'

In reading these lines one might well imagine an echo from Pope's assertion that 'the proper study of mankind is Man' and indeed it is quite likely that Wordsworth had them in mind. On this particular score he had no quarrel with Pope. But it seemed to him that the Augustan poets and philosophers had not pushed their inquiries far enough, that they had not been *sufficiently* realistic. In his Prefaces Wordsworth speaks of himself as first and foremost a psychologist—but one who has learned more of the truth about human nature than the Augustans, with their restricted ideas and their lack of confidence in the resources of the creative imagination, could possibly have done. Wordsworth believed that his duty as a poet was to recall men to that 'filial bond' with nature which alone can produce right feeling and right doing, and alone can bring about a 'wise passiveness', a 'heart that watches and receives', and which can induce

> '. . . That blessed mood
> In which the burden of the mystery,
> In which the heavy and the weary weight
> Of all this unintelligible world
> Is lightened. . .'

Wordsworth's relationship with nature was set forth in loving detail in the greatest autobiographical poems in the language, and though there may have been 'regressive' elements in his attachment to 'Mother Nature' there were also moments of insight into the mysterious regions of instinct, feeling, and the senses that are among the most memorable in English literature. And again it is the *poetry* that carries the revelation *not* the prose sense. This can be strikingly illustrated by placing side by side two passages surprisingly similar as far as their overt Pantheistic content is concerned. One is from Pope's *An Essay on Man*:

> 'All are but part of one stupendous whole,
> Whose body Nature is, and God the soul;
> That charged through all, and yet in all the same;
> Great in the earth, as in the ethereal frame;
> Warms in the sun, refreshes in the breeze,
> Glows in the stars, and blossoms in the trees,
> Lives through all life, extends through all extent,
> Spreads undivided, operates unspent . . .'

Here the 'meaning' is abundantly clear—and yet at the same time it is, imaginatively speaking, meaningless, whereas the second passage, which is from Wordsworth's *Lines composed a few miles above Tintern Abbey, on revisiting the Banks of the Wye during a Tour, July, 1798* superbly render what is completely lacking in the lines from Pope, a feeling of religious exaltation and wonder:

> '. . . A sense sublime
> Of something far more deeply interfused,
> Whose dwelling is the light of setting suns,
> And the round ocean, and the living air,
> And the blue sky, and in the mind of man:
> A motion and a spirit, that impels
> All thinking things, all objects of all thought,
> And rolls through all things.'

The contrast between these two passages is, in effect, the contrast between the Augustans and the Romantics.

All the Romantics of course did not respond to nature as profoundly as Wordsworth, but all of them reveal an appreciation of the relationship between man and his natural background. In some cases it was a fairly simple matter of drawing parallels between the moods and emotions of men and the manifestations of nature—as with Byron and Scott. But in others too nature is the touchstone of mental and spiritual well-being. In Coleridge's *Dejection, an Ode*, for example, it is the inability to respond to the beauties of nature that is symptomatic of a deeper loss, the withering away of the 'shaping spirit of Imagination' which wrings from him the agonizing cry: 'I see, not feel, how beautiful they are.'

Shelley, on the other hand, seeks identification with the elements themselves in his desire to sever the divisions between thought and sensation, while Keats's spiritual and poetic apprenticeship worked itself out through various aspects of nature as deeply as in Wordsworth. In the *Ode to Autumn*, for example, it is through nature that he achieves a concrete realization of sensuous and spiritual *wholeness*.

The turning to nature meant also a turning to the 'natural' in various aspects. There was, for example, the discovery of the special insights of childhood, in which Blake was once again the pioneer, and himself came closest to achieving identification with that envious ability to see 'a World in a grain of sand' which belongs to the child's vision. A poem like *The Tiger* possesses the startling simplicity and the unthinking inward particularity that are to be found in some children's paintings, though Blake in this respect was no 'primitive'. His attitude to childhood was neither naïve nor sentimental: *The Songs of Experience* are implicit in *The Songs of Innocence*, and over both the forbidding shadow of parent, priest, authority lies in wait, all those forces hostile to the kind of knowledge still available to the child, but feared by the conventional adult world. It was his desire to challenge all the established adult values that made Blake value any glimpse of another order of being, whether revealed to him through imagination, hallucination—or participation in the child's mind.

Wordsworth, too, knew the value of the intuitions of childhood, and as he grew older he became more and more poignantly aware of the inroads that time makes upon them, of what he describes as those 'fallings from us, vanishings'. Though some of the country children he depicts in the *Lyrical Ballads* are as stilted and unnatural as their elders, it was when Wordsworth was most in touch with childhood experience—as in *Tintern Abbey*, the most moving passages of *The Prelude*, the *Intimations of Immortality* ode, and the 'Lucy' poems, for example—that he was at his most successful.

This new interest in childhood also found an outlet in prose, for example in some of the writings of Thomas De Quincey, in Charles Lamb's essay *Dream Children*, and in the various books for children which Charles compiled in collaboration with his sister Mary, the most popular of which has been the *Tales from Shakespeare*. At the same time, it must be remembered that this preoccupation was also expressed by writers such as Mrs Anna Letitia Barbauld and Mrs Sarah Trimmer, who were described by Lamb as 'those blights and blasts of childhood' because of the unremitting religiosity and didacticism of their approach. If to these names are added those of other 'improving' writers such as Mrs Mary Sherwood and Hannah More it becomes clear that most of the constituents of the Victorian attitude towards the family as a haven to be protected from all the realities of the world by a wall of relentless piety were in existence long before Queen Victoria came to the throne. It is significant, too, that it was as early as 1818 that Thomas Bowdler published his emasculated *Family Shakespeare*. The truth of the matter is that Blake, Wordsworth, Shelley, Byron, Keats, and their fellows spoke for the intellectuals and the forward-looking spirits of the age: it was people like Hannah More and Thomas Bowdler who spoke for the mass of the middle classes. The heritage of Puritanism in English life and literature could not be dismissed as lightly as all that.

Another symptom of the search for the 'natural' among writers was a new interest in the poorer classes. In the culture of the eighteenth century they had played little part, except as objects of pity or charity, but now it was realized that they represented important areas of human experience and vitality. Although he had tended to transplant his own sophisticated notions among his rustic characters Wordsworth performed a valuable service in drawing attention to this fact, while George Crabbe's poems presented a more realistic picture of rustic life. The advent of semi-educated poets such as Robert Bloomfield and John Clare was also probably related to this new realization.

The greatest of all the 'ploughboy poets', however, was Robert Burns. Although he exaggerated his illiteracy in the service of the Romantic image, there could be no doubt that the characters portrayed in his poems, whether honest labourers, vagabonds, or ne'er-do-wells, were drawn from intimate personal experience. At the same time they possessed the added advantage—from the English Romantics' point of view—of coming from a picturesque region far from London, and one that the Augustans had regarded as on the dubious fringes of 'society'. In addition, Burns's love lyrics revived the note of passionate personal utterance lost for so long, while the circumstances of his life made him, almost as much as Byron, a prototype of the Romantic poet and—again almost as much as Byron—an outcast from polite society.

In all these respects Burns was one of the chief pioneers of the Romantic Revival. His *Poems, Chiefly in the Scottish Dialect*, published in 1786, were, moreover, part of a tradition of

Scottish dialect poetry already firmly established by such poets as Allan Ramsay (linking the seventeenth and eighteenth centuries) and Robert Fergusson, who died some twelve years before the appearance of Burns's volume. Burns in consequence, unlike Blake whose *Songs of Innocence* were published three years later, was not a voice crying in the wilderness as far as his fellow-countrymen were concerned. As for his readers south of the Border his language and metres exercised a strong appeal upon ears jaded by Augustan diction and already stimulated by the measures of Macpherson and Percy.

It is indeed only when he was close to his native tradition that Burns was a great poet: when he tried to write in polite English he became just another conventional eighteenth-century poet. It was the use of the vernacular, both in short lyrics and in longer satirical or narrative poems, that was his great strength, while in some of his love poems he was also working over traditional ballad material. At the same time Burns's genius submitted the Scottish dialect to a poetic transmutation, so that although in his great poems there is nothing to offend a Scot, a sufficient number of English forms remain for them to be enjoyed without difficulty by English readers who have never visited Scotland or heard Scots spoken. Burns's practice, in fact, by demonstrating that the 'language really used by men' *can* be used as the basis of great poetry, might be regarded as the natural corollary to Wordsworth's theory.

The closer to the vernacular tradition the better the poetry, is a generalization that can also be applied to Burns's contemporaries and successors, and it is particularly true in the case of Sir Walter Scott, whose lengthy narrative poems written in English —such as *The Lay of the Last Minstrel*—are far less important than the collection of Scottish ballads that he made, and the songs he himself wrote in the spirit of the old ballads—such as *Proud Maisie*. This fine poem appears in *The Heart of Midlothian*—and it was in this and other novels dealing with Scottish history that Scott came close to achieving in prose what Burns had achieved in poetry—a synthesizing of English and genuine Scots in order to create a universally convincing form of utterance. For it is above all their vivid, racy speech that endows characters like Jeanie Deans in *The Heart of Midlothian* with such abundant vitality.

Maria Edgeworth performed for Ireland something of the same service that Burns and Scott had performed for Scotland. Her

A page from William Blake's *Songs of Innocence*, 1789

Horace Walpole's library at Strawberry Hill

novels of Irish country life introduced real peasants and made them speak in a genuine Irish idiom. In *Castle Rackrent*, for example, it is through the eyes and the colloquial speech of Thady Quirk, the old steward of the Rackrent family, that the reader comes to know the hard-drinking Sir Patrick, the law-suiting Sir Murtagh, the irascible Sir Kit, and the improvidently generous Sir Condy. Though her novels were marred by the same rigid didacticism that attended her writings for children, Maria Edgeworth's studies of Irish manners and characters have something of the vividness of Jane Austen. It was their 'rich humour, pathetic tenderness, and admirable tact', Scott confessed, that led him to novel writing. On the other hand, the Irish quality of Moore's ballads belongs to English drawing-rooms rather than to the Irish countryside.

The desire to get away from the conventional centre of society to its periphery also helps to explain the attraction of faraway places, an interest furthered by the discoveries of Captain James Cook, and by the expansion of the East Indian trade and the penetration of the Indian sub-continent. Foreign parts had exercised an appeal in the Augustan period too—as witness the tremendous popularity of *Robinson Crusoe*. But the fascination of Defoe's novel lay above all in Crusoe's efforts to transplant 'society' as he knew it upon his desert island. For the Romantics the attraction of distant places lay in their remoteness from 'polite' control, in the strangeness of their social customs, and in the apparently superior spontaneity of their inhabitants. Hence the great vogue for exotic settings.

But there was more to it than the production of highly coloured backcloths. The voyaging to strange places and the accidents that befall the traveller were often used as symbols for the dangers and distresses that wait upon the traveller through life itself—as in Cowper's *The Task* and in Coleridge's *The Ancient Mariner*. The relaxation of social and emotional controls and the break-up of the old disciplines, leading to a good deal of mental tension, meant, moreover, that the 'countries of the mind' which the Romantic writer explored were themselves often exotic and remote, haunted by strange and sometimes nightmarish shapes.

Indeed travelling itself was in many cases a psychological necessity, instead of being—as in the days of the aristocratic 'Grand Tour'—part of a gentleman's preparation for 'society'. It was an inner restlessness, for example, that started the famous Lady Hester Stanhope on her wanderings in the Middle East in 1811, while in Byron's case the urge to retreat from the centre of society was carried to a logical extreme of ostracism and exile. The characters of his plays and narrative poems—Childe Harold, Manfred, Cain, and all the others—are in one form or another the outcasts of society, and as Scott pointed out they are all the same character repeated over and over again—for the simple reason that they were all fundamentally self-portraits. What is significant, however, is that these constant repetitions did not pall upon the public: indeed it was Byron's resounding success that drove Scott out of the market as far as narrative poetry was concerned. The truth of the matter was that Byron both in the circumstances of his life and in his poetry acted as a kind of Romantic scapegoat. He could be at one and the same time an object of execration—as the symbol of the disorder and lawlessness the middle classes feared (the very opposite of the Augustan virtues)—and, at the level of wishful-thinking, an expression of their secret desires. His readers were able to howl him down as an anti-Christ at the same time that they clamoured at the book-shops for copies of his latest verses. The ambivalence of his own attitude towards the culture of the Augustans merely increased his effectiveness in this respect. The impiety of the poet who could, in Canto I of *Don Juan* (1819), proclaim his literary allegiance in the form of a parody of the Creed:

'Thou shalt believe in Milton, Dryden, Pope;
Thou shalt not set up Wordsworth, Coleridge, Southey . . .'

pointed at least to an underlying appreciation of the values against which, in other respects, he was in revolt: the rebel in fact was no root-and-branch anarchist like Shelley, but proceeded from an accepted basis. He was the kind of Romantic the English most needed—and most needed to reject. And although Byron indulged in a good deal of posturing, the poetry written after he had accepted exile, together with his brilliantly intelligent correspondence carry the impression of a man who was aware of the role he was called upon to fill and convinced of its value for—and therefore fundamentally of its attachment to—the society of his time.

Byron's potency as a symbol and prototype of Romanticism is proved by his tremendous influence abroad. The political aspect is of course important, for it was Byron's active involvement, on the side of liberal and liberating ideas, in many of the great European political issues of the day (and particularly in the causes of Italian and Greek independence) that above all saved his exile from degenerating into a sterile theatrical gesture and gave it a wider relevance. The Byronic heroes who proliferated in European fiction were expressions both of psychological stresses and of political aspirations.

In addition to Byron's outcasts there were Wordsworth's tramps, Burns's ne'er-do-wells, and the vagabonds of Scott's novels such as Madge Wildfire. A general sympathy with those normally regarded as beyond the social pale was in fact one of the most strongly marked features of the Romantic Revival. Like all the other symptoms of the movement away from the social norm it was in essence a reflection of the desire to belittle the authority of the social group and therefore to stress the validity of individual judgments whether they clashed with conventional opinion or not. A natural development here was that autobiographical writing became more personal—as in Wordsworth's *The Prelude*, Leigh Hunt's *Autobiography*, and the frank, intimate tone of Lamb's 'Elia' essays and of the essays of Hazlitt (in such marked contrast to the polite, social approach of the eighteenth-century essayists). At times the intimacy of autobiography took on the journalistic air of 'shocking revelations'—as in Thomas De Quincey's *Confessions of an English Opium Eater* (though this and other of De Quincey's books also contained some richly evocative prose). It should be noted, however, that the taking of opium, along with other forms of outrageous anti-social behaviour, was itself symptomatic of the Romantic revolt against conformity, though it also bore witness to the sufferings of sensitive minds in a period of stress and rapid change. It is no mere coincidence that such a comparatively high proportion of the writers from the beginnings of the break-up of Augustan security onwards suffered from melancholia or insanity, the extremist form of 'alienation'—the examples of Christopher Smart, Gray, Clare, Cowper, Coleridge, and Charles and Mary Lamb immediately spring to mind.

Although Romanticism can be seen in some of its aspects as a further manifestation of the individualism released by the Renaissance it contained little of the humanist classicism, apart from exceptions like Walter Savage Landor and Thomas Love Peacock. Keats's warm, sensuous response to ancient Greece, for example, was the reverse of the neo-classical attitude of the Augustans, and there was a strong impulse to turn to periods as remote as possible from the eighteenth century.

It was the Middle Ages in particular that appeared to offer the greatest contrast to the Age of Reason. The Romantic approach to them, it is true, had more of fantasy to it than historical accuracy.

English Literature

It was a 'picture-book' medievalism, but it gave Romantic literature some of its outstanding successes. There was, for example, Keats's *The Eve of St Agnes* with its brilliantly concrete realization of detail and atmosphere; and there was Coleridge's unfinished *Christabel* which contained the same hypnotic power that distinguished *The Ancient Mariner* and the magical fragment, *Kubla Khan; or A Vision in a Dream*.

The 'sense of wonder' in Coleridge's poem was a more sophisticated version of the fashionable *frissons* attending the Gothic cult. This manifested itself in architecture as well as in literature, and notably in the mock-Gothic mansions of Horace Walpole and William Beckford at Strawberry Hill and Fonthill respectively. The interest of these buildings lay not so much in their aesthetic aspects as in the opportunities they afforded for shadowy and mysterious atmosphere. Walpole exploited these to the full in *The Castle of Otranto*—which appearing as early as 1764 was one of the harbingers of Romanticism—in which 'sub-terraneous regions', 'intricate cloisters', and the sounds of creaking doors echoing through a 'long labyrinth of darkness' conspire to produce in the heroine's mind 'every suggestion that horror could inspire'.

In the Gothic novel therefore medievalism was equated with mystery and terror. The most considerable successors to Walpole's novel were Ann Radcliffe's *The Mysteries of Udolpho* and Matthew Gregory Lewis's *The Monk*, while Beckford's oriental novel *Vathek* and Charles Maturin's *Melmoth the Wanderer* were related to the *genre*—thoroughly satirized by Jane Austen in *Northanger Abbey*.

There was a good deal of pseudo-medievalism too in Scott's novels *Ivanhoe* and *The Talisman*, and generally speaking he was at his best in dealing with periods closer to his own times: thus *Waverley*, his first novel (1814), *Rob Roy*, and *The Heart of Midlothian* were set in the eighteenth century, while the action of *Guy Mannering* and *The Antiquary* belonged to the period of Scott's own childhood and youth, and it was only with *Old Mortality*, the fine novel about the Scottish Covenanters of the seventeenth century, that he really became a 'historical' novelist with genuine powers of historical insight and perspective. It is also noticeable that the novels set outside Scotland are inferior to those rooted in his native soil. On the other hand, it is important to remember that it was novels like *Ivanhoe* and *Quentin Durward* that had the greatest influence upon the development of the historical novel, not only in Britain but in European countries as far afield as Russia, where Scott had many followers.

Scott's relationship to the Romantics, however, like that of Byron, was a somewhat equivocal one. Politically and emotionally he was a conservative who had little sympathy with the extravagant or revolutionary aspects of Romanticism. It was indeed disgust with its Whiggism that caused him to stop contributing to the *Edinburgh Review* and to throw his weight behind the Tory *Quarterly Review*.

These two publications, together with *Blackwood's Edinburgh Magazine*, formed a powerful nucleus of opinion—how powerful can be seen by the fact that the *Edinburgh Review* reached a circulation of fourteen thousand copies—and the important point about them is that, whatever their disagreements politically, in cultural matters they were devoted to the older eighteenth-century standards of good sense and decorum. Most of the Romantic poets —and notably Byron, Keats, and Wordsworth—were attacked in their columns.

This was one of the reasons that drove Wordsworth and Coleridge to propound their views in Prefaces, though the Romantics had other platforms for their views. One of these was the public lecture, and to this popular institution of the times English criticism owes some of its liveliest manifestations. Coleridge's lectures on Shakespeare marked the high-water mark —and also struck a powerful blow in the critical war between Classicists and Romanticists. Strongly influenced by the German critics Lessing, Schlegel, and J. P. Richter—who in their reaction against the classical doctrines of the French theatre had set up Shakespeare as the dramatic ideal—Coleridge effectively reversed the Augustan evaluation, arguing that far from being an 'untutored genius' ignorant of 'the Rules' Shakespeare, like nature herself, created not mechanically but organically, so that all the elements, including the mixture of comedy and tragedy which had struck the Augustans as particularly reprehensible, were fused into a harmonious whole. It is from assumptions such as these that a good deal of twentieth-century Shakespearian criticism has proceeded.

The rejection of the formalistic approach by the Romantics also led to a freer play of the imagination in dramatic criticism, particularly in speculation about 'character'. In the cases of Hazlitt (who lectured on the characters of Shakespeare's plays and on other subjects) and of Coleridge, this produced some extremely shrewd observations, but it was also to lead to one of the worst faults of Victorian criticism of Shakespeare—the tendency to submit characters to a process of sentimental fantasy, as if they existed quite apart from the plays to which they belonged.

While Coleridge, Hazlitt, De Quincey, and others freed Shakespeare from the shackles of Augustan prejudice Charles Lamb inaugurated a vogue for Shakespeare's contemporaries with his *Specimens of the English Dramatic Poets contemporary with Shakespeare* which were accompanied by useful and sometimes brilliant commentaries. He adopted a similar approach for other aspects of English literature, and on the whole it was those periods and writers who afforded the greatest contrast to the Age of Reason that most aroused his sympathies. It was Lamb who was largely responsible for the revival of interest in the tragedy of blood and revenge of Webster and Tourneur: a service of mixed value, for two of its by-products, Shelley's *The Cenci* and Thomas Lovell Beddoes's *Death's Jest Book, or the Fool's Tragedy*, in spite of some effective passages, can properly be considered as examples of the Romantic decadence.

Outside the periodicals the most formidable critic of the Romantics was Thomas Love Peacock, a passionate though good-natured Hellenist. He satirized many of the Romantic writers and their styles of writing (notably in *Nightmare Abbey*), but he was also a writer of the great comic tradition who transcended ephemeral issues. His favourite device was to assemble a group of characters —rich in foible and eccentricity—in a country-house environment and, in the course of much good eating and drinking, to allow them to ride their various hobby-horses through the medium of direct conversation, which often leaves the narrative framework altogether and is set out in play-form. Peacock's methods (which have some affinities to those of Sterne) have been followed in many important respects by some of the most original of the writers of the twentieth century, notably by Aldous Huxley (especially in *Crome Yellow*), Ronald Firbank and (with grimmer overtones) Ivy Compton-Burnett. The tone of Peacock's dialogue is also similar in many respects to that of George Bernard Shaw, particularly in *Heartbreak House*. Peacock's novels indeed came closer to the essence of comic dramatic dialogue than anything actually composed for the theatre, for although many of the Romantic poets tried their hands at drama they achieved little success, and in fact the theatre of the period relied to a considerable extent upon adaptations of novels.

There were elements in Jane Austen's work too which might have made her novels suitable for such a purpose, and which indeed in another age might have made her a great comic dramatist. In *Pride and Prejudice* and *Northanger Abbey*, for example, there are passages, and sometimes whole chapters, which consist almost entirely of dialogue and which have the point and tempo of scenes from a play. Her humour had something in common with that of Peacock, and the social values with which she was concerned related her to the tradition which he represented. The ironical treatment of Marianne in *Sense and Sensibility*, for example, shows what she thought of the release of the emotions advocated by the Romantics. It is, in fact, plainly contrary to her own view that strong impulses and feelings must be subjected to the control of good sense and good taste, not only for the sake of the individual concerned as out of consideration for the social group. That is why so often in her novels the heroine at moments of stress retires to grapple with the agitations of spirit in solitude, and why even close intimates are shown as possessing considerable private reticences and as forbearing either to demand or obtrude confidences. The ideal is of the kind of reserve and consideration for others that belong to a life lived in public—and it is a very Augustan one.

At the same time, in Jane Austen's novels—as indeed in so much Augustan literature—the feelings are there: the restraint is exercised upon a reality and not, as happened with many of her Victorian imitators, upon a shadow, so that in the one case there is constant vitality and in the other a uniform insipidity. It would be wrong, however, to think of Jane Austen as an anachronism, an author born too late and dealing with a way of life that has gone. For one thing the society she portrays shows all the symptoms of vigorous actuality: there is nothing in the least *fin de siècle* about it. For another the characters whom Jane Austen places so exactly in a so carefully observed social context transcend their bounds to become, like all characters in great literature, figures of as timeless and universal a significance as the pilgrims of Chaucer. The part played by individualism, moreover, is greater in Jane Austen than is sometimes realized. In nearly all her novels there is a heroine of superior intelligence and moral fibre who is called upon to make individual judgments, and though these are certainly related to the society to which she belongs they are not always acceptable to it. This is particularly so where love is concerned: the heroine's circle may give its blessing to marriage for money or social standing, but the heroine always knows—or as with Anne Elliot in *Persuasion* comes to know—that this is an issue in which she must be guided by her own feelings alone and not by the 'prudent counsels' of others. The ideal of love as the only basis for marriage is in fact absolutely central to Jane Austen's morality, and the independence and determination with which she expresses it through her heroines are not really in line with the Augustan ideal of strict social conformity. In this sense, therefore, Jane Austen too gave expression to the reaction against ready-made codes and to the assertion of the sanctity of individual responsibility and judgment which were such important aspects of the Romantic Revival.

The truth of the matter was that Jane Austen, like Peacock, Walter Savage Landor, Samuel Rogers, and the other convinced 'Classicists' of the period, belonged wholly to her own times, and was just as much a representative of the Romantic Revival as Wordsworth or Shelley or Keats. For Classicists and Romanticists needed each other, and it was the fruitful tension between the two scales of values that helped to produce so much great work. In a wider sense indeed this is true of all the great periods of English literature. Although on the whole its natural temper has been more 'romantic' than 'classical', the values implicit in Classicism have of course been present too. Classical restraint, harmony, proportion, and form indeed are just as much in evidence in the best of Romantic literature as in the best of Augustan. It was only the inferior writers who turned the new psychological insights of the great Romantics upside-down and indulged in the sentimental, the sensational, the morbid, the occult, or the erotic. In any case these faults were no worse than those of frigidity, pomposity, and empty rhetoric that sprang from the attempts made from the sixteenth century onwards to 'imitate' the classics. Romanticism and Classicism represent two different but complementary modes of human existence, and both will inevitably be reflected in literature. But a truly living literature is not created out of ready-made rules or formulae no matter what the label attached to them.

The fault of a good deal of Victorian and Edwardian literature was that it did to a large extent rely upon such formulae. Although there were many instances of hollow and academic classicizing it was admittedly the short-cuts and facile responses extracted from Romanticism that were to prove the most dangerous to poetry— and it is in this connexion that John Keats occupies a unique position in the history of the Romantic Revival and of English

View of the west and south fronts of Fonthill Abbey, the home of William Beckford

John Keats by Joseph Severn, 1821

poetry generally. For it was his work that exhibited both the worst and the best aspects of Romanticism. He of all the Romantics was the most passionately dedicated to poetry, the most thoroughly 'the poet'; he was revered as such by the Victorians—but too often for the wrong reasons; and yet at the same time he reveals more completely perhaps than any English writer since Shakespeare that the essence of true poetry lies in the synthesis of fantasy and reality achieved through suffering and self-knowledge.

When *Blackwood's Edinburgh Magazine* in its series 'On the Cockney School of Poetry' attacked both Keats's 1817 volume of poems and his *Endymion: A Poetic Romance* it had considerable justification. Keats's early poetry did contain numerous vulgarities; and the Leigh Hunt circle was in many respects a dangerous portent for English literature. Keats indeed began writing under the worst possible auspices: for at the outset he was very much a 'literary' poet and his models were nearly all such as to increase the tendency.

But the most remarkable thing about Keats was his capacity for self-criticism and self-education. He was quite right when he said that none of the critics could have been more acutely aware of the faults of his verse than he was himself. Thus in his Preface to *Endymion* he wrote of 'great inexperience, immaturity, and every error denoting a feverish attempt, rather than a deed accomplished'. He knew perfectly well that the over-sweetness and mawkishness of his early poetry was the result of immaturity.

The same clarity of critical perception lay behind his abandonment of *Hyperion* because (he wrote to his friend Reynolds) 'there were too many Miltonic inversions in it. Miltonic verse cannot be written but in an artful, or rather artist's humour. I wish to give myself up to other sensations.' And in another letter to his brother in America he recognized that Milton's language was a magnificent expression of his own personality and genius, but that as a model for other English writers it must be ranked as 'a foreign idiom ... a corruption of our language'. 'Life to him', Keats declared, 'would be death to me'—and again there is the significant conclusion: 'Miltonic verse cannot be written but is the verse of art. I wish to devote myself to another verse alone.'

The story of Keats's development, as chronicled not only in his poetry but also in his letters—the most astonishing record of a poet's apprenticeship and 'self-analysis' in the English language—is above all one of weaning himself from 'the artist's humour' from 'the verse of art' in order to embody 'other sensations' in 'another

verse alone', in order, that is, to express the truths of his own experience and not merely to adopt the Romantic gestures or to
go through the motions of some abstract conception of 'Poesy'.

At first it had seemed to Keats that the kind of poetic truth he
was searching for could be found in the simple assertion of the
superiority of the senses over the intellect. 'Oh for a life of Sensations rather than of thoughts!' he exclaimed in one of his early
letters, and his main concern at this stage was with the degree to
which poetry could register the immediacy of sensation. In spite of
the many faults of the early poems they do reveal something of that
'delight in richness and sweetness of sound even to a faulty excess'
which Coleridge argued, in connexion with Shakespeare's early
poems, is symptomatic of authentic youthful genius.

Even at this stage, moreover, Keats can be seen struggling to
make his idea of 'intensity' embody something more than a simple
surrender to sensuous delights. As he matured under the pressure
of harsh personal experience so his concept of 'intensity' deepened.
For the poet he believed *all* experiences, from the simplest to the
most complex, must be 'felt upon the pulses' before they can be
transmuted into art. But to render the insights of suffering calls for
very different instruments and a very different approach from
those needed for simple sensation. This was the problem he was
still grappling with when he died. Nevertheless in the great odes
and in the revised *Hyperion* he reached a maturity that few other
English poets have achieved. Behind them lay the realization that
the ugliness and misery of life must be faced without the comfort
of being able to see any 'balance of good and evil'. They embodied
Keats's concept of 'Negative Capability', the quality which it
seemed to him Shakespeare 'possessed so enormously'—the frame
of mind, that is, 'when one is capable of being in uncertainties,
mysteries, doubts, without any irritable reaching after fact and
reason. . .' And what indeed is so striking about this final phase
in Keats's development is that in the face of the most acute
perception of the world's sufferings as well as of his own, he still
refused any 'irritable reaching after' an 'abstract philosophy', or
any surrender to the ready-made avenues of escape offered by
Romanticism.

The seductions of the Romantic formulae at war with the
inexorable demands of reality indeed constituted one of Keats's
major themes and produced some of the most fruitful tensions in
his poetry. In the *Ode on a Grecian Urn*, for example, the 'stillness',
the immunity to time and suffering of the urn is brought into

contrast with the actuality of the poet's experience. The *Ode on Melancholy*, too, sets up against an academic, self-indulgent grief, supported by the Gothic trappings of 'wolf's bane' and 'night-shade', the bitter realization that real suffering 'dwells with Beauty —Beauty that must die'.

It is, however, in the *Ode to a Nightingale* that the issue is most powerfully stated. Here Keats eagerly and often desperately explores the efficacy of various forms of escape, to be brought up every time against the knowledge that for the genuine poet there *are* no short-cuts. Thus the desire to follow the nightingale:

> '. . . and leave the world unseen
> And with thee fade away into the forest dim'

is quickly frustrated by the contemplation of:

> 'The weariness, the fever and the fret
> Here, where men sit and hear each other groan;
> Where palsy shakes a few, sad, last gray hairs,
> Where youth grows pale, and spectre thin, and dies.'

The 'magic casements' of Romantic fantasy are no more efficacious, and there is a particular poignancy in the discovery:

> '. . . the fancy cannot cheat so well
> As she is fam'd to do, deceiving elf.'

For of all the poets of the period none had surrendered himself more whole-heartedly to the Romantic seductions, the 'shadows haunting faerily the brain' with 'triumphs gay of old romance', and none had dedicated himself more thoroughly to the Romantic image of the 'Poet'. That 'the viewless wings of Poesy' were no more effective than 'Bacchus and his pards' in the face of real experience must have been a particularly painful discovery. But the rejection of 'Poesy', of the idea that poetry was a separate province remote from the harsh realities of living, demanding a separate voice and a separate poetic stance, is the most important thing about Keats's poetry. It meant that the most representative of all the Romantic poets was in a sense anti-Romantic—that is, that he had reacted powerfully against those elements in Romanticism which led in the direction of Aestheticism and the Ivory Tower. It was not his fault that so many of his later admirers failed to appreciate the fact.

6 · Victorians and Moderns

THE world and Britain's place in it have changed so much since Queen Victoria came to the throne in 1837 that to bring Victorians and Moderns together under one heading seems (to adapt Dr Johnson's description of the imagery of the Metaphysical poets) like linking the contraries of a time-scale by violence together. And yet the Victorians are still very close to us.

The truth of the matter is that the basic problem which underlay the ceaseless 'Victorian debate' has been and still is the overriding problem of our times. This problem can be described as fundamentally religious, moral, cultural, economic, or psychological according to personal predilections: but whatever the label it has not altered since Thomas Carlyle as long ago as 1829 wrote in *Signs of the Times*: 'Not the external and physical alone is now managed by machinery, but the spiritual also. . . For the same habit regulates not our modes of action alone, but our modes of thought and feeling. Men are grown mechanical in head and heart, as well as in hand.'

In other words, the challenge that has faced men since the dawn of the 'machine age' has been that of bringing to life a significance beyond that of the 'cash nexus', of preserving the humane values it threatened, and of trying to ensure that emotional maturity kept pace with commercial and technological developments.

Many of the Romantic poets—and Wordsworth above all—were aware of this challenge, and what is more they countered it with positive contributions, emphasizing those qualities of heart, spirit, and imagination that are the only antidotes. The main criticism that can be levelled against the Victorian poets is that, on the whole, they did not face up to it with anything like the same insight or determination—and it is here that the contrast outlined in the last chapter between Keats's profound and dynamic examination of Beauty and Truth as it affected actual living, and the loose 'Romantic' interpretation of the phrase becomes most significant.

It can be studied best of all in the case of Alfred, Lord Tennyson, whose preoccupation with verbal felicity has something in common with Pope's. The passage from *The Dunciad* quoted in an earlier chapter and ending with the line 'Love-whispering woods, and lute-resounding waves', for example, has much the same careful search for mellifluous effect as the opening stanza of the Choric Song in Tennyson's *The Lotos Eaters*, which was the most important poem in his 1833 volume:

> 'There is sweet music here that softer falls
> Than petals from blown roses on the grass,
> Or night-dews on still waters between walls
> Of shadowy granite, in a gleaming pass;
> Music that gentlier on the spirit lies,
> Than tir'd eyelids upon tir'd eyes;
> Music that brings sweet sleep down from the blissful skies.
> Here are cool mosses deep,
> And through the moss the ivies creep,
> And in the stream the long-leaved flowers weep,
> And from the craggy ledge the poppy hangs in sleep.'

The verbal magic of these lines demanded a sensitivity to words that only a very genuine poet can command. Tennyson possessed it to such a degree that it can often lull uneasiness on other scores.

The Lotos Eaters as a whole is obviously the work of a Victorian Romantic—and just as obviously of one deeply indebted to Keats. But the elements in Keats's poetry upon which Tennyson drew were not those of his mature achievement, and were indeed the very ones which Keats himself regarded as inadequate and which he was struggling to transform into a deeper and more comprehensive vision. Keats's absorption in nature, for example, was one of the avenues towards the exploration of the senses as a way of extending his experience and understanding of life, whereas in Tennyson's case one too often feels it was an escape from those aspects of Victorian England which, as a true artist, he secretly hated but could not overcome. As a consequence while even in his most self-indulgent moments of nature worship Keats's sense of actuality was still strong, Tennyson, in spite of the photographic exactitude of bud, leaf, or feather, throws over his natural description a veil of dreamy nostalgia and melancholy.

He belonged, indeed, to an age which had a particular liking for generalizations such as 'Beauty and Truth' and which preferred its poets to leave them undefined. One of the outstanding characteristics of the poetry of the Victorians was its proneness to fasten grandiose themes upon vague Romantic notions and an equally vague and often second-hand Romantic vocabulary.

Tennyson, as a matter of fact, showed signs of being well aware that the role of Victorian Poet Laureate was irreconcilable with the promptings of the true artist and that he suffered from the realization. There is, for example, a vehemence of utterance and even a suggestion of Byronic defiance in *Locksley Hall*, while in *Maud* there are elements of harsh satire and even passion. There is the anguish of a divided mind, too, in *The Two Voices*, and Tennyson was usually at his best when he faced at least some part of the reality of his environment and allowed his feelings of frustration, failure, or regret to fuse naturally with his technical skill and sensitivity.

At first sight it might appear that this element of defeat, which is a common characteristic of Victorian poetry, was absent from the work of the 'optimistic' Robert Browning. It is certainly true that he was one of the few poets of the age who dared express simple joys and passions and even acknowledge the existence of the body, and the poems in which he does so are his best and most durable.

If Browning had devoted his very considerable talents to the exploration of his emotional and sensuous promptings, indeed, he might have become the one poet to rise above the age. For the truly great poet never merely subscribes to or even 'expresses' the age to which he belongs: in some way he is always above it, always a man 'born out of his time'. Browning, however, sank back into Victorianism as surely as did Tennyson—and it was the contemporary taste for moral casuistry that proved his fatal temptation. At the beginning (partly under the influence of Byron and Shelley) it looked as if he might avoid the worst dangers: thus his claim that in *Pauline: A Fragment of a Confession* (1833) he was 'exploring passion and mind' has some justification, chiefly because he was dealing with personal experience. *Paracelsus*, too, contained an exciting promise—that the theme of the charlatan would produce an ironic awareness of the role the poet was expected to play in Victorian culture—but it remained a promise only. And soon he was specializing in the *genre* of the dramatic monologue which brought him contemporary fame and culminated in the complex multiple-form of *The Ring and the Book* (1868). Most of these monologues suffer from the common Victorian fault of bringing a rhetorical sledge-hammer to crack an intellectual nut. The manner is impressive, the twists and turns of the debate are always ingenious, but today these poems are as dated as the heavy volumes of Victorian sermons on provincial second-hand bookstalls. They illustrate the common Victorian assumption that solemnity is the same thing as seriousness, a confusion which manifested itself in many spheres of Victorian life, including its mock-Gothic architecture and the monstrous stuffiness of its drawing-rooms. Although Browning claimed that his chief interest was in 'the incidents in the development of a soul' he never really faced up to the complexities such a claim implied, and one cannot avoid the suspicion that the various characters about whom he wrote were really a series of masks behind which he continually dodged in order to avoid looking too deeply into his own soul or into the realities of his times. Certainly the voices that proceed from behind them, in spite of their colloquial free-and-easiness, are often irritatingly distorted, and when one reads most of these monologues one longs to hear again—as in the lyrics—the natural speaking voice of the author. It was as if Browning held in his hands the great gift of words and instead of bending it to its proper purposes twisted it into all kinds of contorted shapes. In studying the age, indeed, the feeling of resources of language lying about unused or used in ways incommensurate with the available energy and vitality is always present. The fondness for punning, 'Nonsense Verse', and various games with language, particularly associated with the names of Edward Lear, Lewis Carroll, and W. S. Gilbert, is one of the many symptoms.

As one follows the course of Victorian poetry similar reservations have to be made time after time. Thus Matthew Arnold, one of the most important of the 'new voices' of the 1850s, despite the eminent readability of his verse, leaves the impression of having written poetry well below the level of his very considerable abilities. As a classicist he set himself against what he regarded as the over-decoration of Tennyson. But he too was indebted to Keats—and again in the wrong way. *The Scholar Gipsy*, for example, leans strongly upon the movement of Keats's *Ode to Autumn*, without recapturing its firmness or richness of texture. Arnold, too, like Keats in his apprenticeship, was very much a 'literary' poet. His talent was sufficiently strong to re-create these influences in original forms—though a slightly academic, scholarly flavour often remains. There is of course nothing wrong in literary indebtedness: nevertheless Victorian poetry as a whole is far more 'literary' than that of the great periods, and an excess of derivativeness has to be reckoned among its weaknesses. As far as poetry is concerned it is usually one of the symptoms of low vitality.

Arnold's charm consists chiefly in a stoic solitariness, tempered by a certain wry humour. Some of his poems—and notably *Dover Beach*, one of the best poems of the era—squarely faced the issues that agitated the age in which he lived. But generally speaking the question remains—where is the force and energy that made a prose work like *Culture and Anarchy* so relevant to the spirit of the times that even Count Tolstoy far away in Russia admired it?

Even the movements that were consciously directed against the 'benumbing round' of the age (as Arnold called it) for the most part petered out unsatisfactorily, or turned into unproductive by-roads. Some of the pronouncements in *The Germ: Thoughts towards Nature in Poetry, Literature, and Art*, the periodical in which the Pre-Raphaelite Brotherhood in 1850 set out their programme, have an almost revolutionary ring. There was, for instance, the determination to make art serve a social purpose 'by a firm attachment to truth in every point of representation'. But in practice this chiefly meant a retreat into a sentimentalized medievalism, and as far as poetry was concerned the dominant influence was again that of Keats—and once again those aspects of his work that were the most 'literary', the most closely associated with 'Poesy'. The medieval trappings of *The Eve of St Agnes*, the embroidery of *Isabella*, and the pseudo-balladry of *La Belle Dame Sans Merci* exercised a particularly potent spell upon the Pre-Raphaelite poets.

This is not to deny that Rossetti wrote poetry of an original and distinctive tone and atmosphere—but it was not the kind of poetry which Keats and the other great Romantics wrote at their best, poetry which revealed new and startling insights and which in its total intention unequivocally challenged the more materialistic aspects of their age. And here an important generalization must be made—that whereas before the Romantic Revival, poetry (and especially dramatic poetry) for the most part acted as the spearhead or advance-guard to the dynamic of the age, from the Romantic Revival onwards the task that poetry has been mainly called upon to fulfil has been that of *opposing* the prevailing current. One of the criticisms that can justly be made against the majority of the Victorian poets is that though they were often aware of this fact they did so little of positive value about it.

Even the socialist William Morris (also associated with the Pre-Raphaelites), though he wrote a good deal of eminently readable poetry and performed a valuable service in translating some of the Scandinavian sagas as well as the Anglo-Saxon epic poem *Beowulf*, subscribed, in the 'Apology' to *The Earthly Paradise*

The name of Dante Gabriel Rossetti is heard for the first time in the United States
of America. Time: 1881. Lecturer: Mr Oscar Wilde.
A caricature by Max Beerbohm

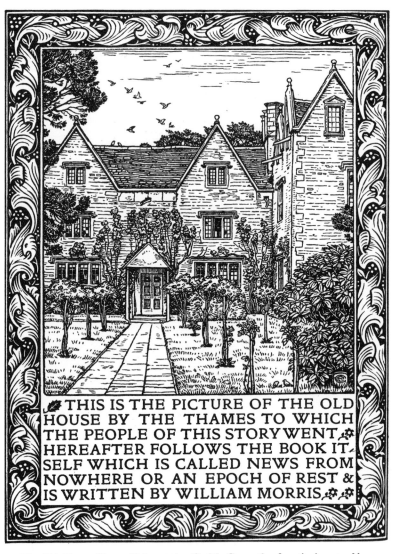

The Old Manor House, Kelmscott by C. M. Gare, the frontispiece to *News from Nowhere* by William Morris (Kelmscott Press, 1892)

(1868–70), to the prevailing idea that the poet was no more than a 'dreamer of dreams', the 'singer of an empty day'.

In spite, however, of their essential escapism the Pre-Raphaelites, because of their 'realism' and the sensuous nature of their imagery, which earned them the label of 'the fleshly school', aroused a good deal of shocked protest. So, too, did the appearance in 1859 of the famous *Rubáiyát of Omar Khayyám*, translated (or rather adapted) by Edward Fitzgerald, with its intoxicating rhythms and hedonistic delight in love, wine, and poetry. But the greatest shock of all was administered by *The Poems and Ballads* of Algernon Charles Swinburne, which were influenced by Baudelaire's *Les Fleurs du Mal*. There are certainly many signs of revolt in Swinburne. There was, for example, the extreme republicanism inspired by Shelley and Victor Hugo; there was the determined paganism that proclaimed the superiority of the cult of Venus over that of 'the pale Galilean', the defiant blasphemy of his 'Glory to Man in the highest! for Man is the master of things', and there was the sensuality of imagery and metre. In addition Swinburne with his enthusiasm for contemporary French writers—as well as for Villon, Aristophanes, Catullus, and the seventeenth-century English dramatists—was an important agent in modifying Victorian insularity and in extending the range of literary reference. What is more, there was a new vitality in Swinburne's versification. And yet in spite of all this he achieved no revolutionary break-through. His many literary and intellectual interests and his metrical vigour and variety were in advance of his experience and of his poetic vision. He was fundamentally an immature poet, as he was an immature personality, and like most of the other Victorians he subscribed to a withdrawal from life.

George Meredith's series of poems entitled *Modern Love*, which presented the reverse side of the matrimonial picture of Coventry Patmore's *The Angel in the House*, outraged his contemporaries of the 1860s almost as much as Swinburne's *Poems and Ballads*. They certainly introduced something of the bite of truth and realism, and some critics have seen in Meredith the most original and forward-looking of the Victorian poets. But both poetic pressure and technique are variable, and though the nature poems contain effective passages they are marred by the common Victorian-Romantic diffuseness and are usually overloaded with grandiose philosophical speculations which, whatever their intention, have little in common with Wordsworth's poetically realized 'philosophy' of nature.

English Literature

The aesthetic movement of the 1890s incorporated the influences of Pre-Raphaelitism, Swinburne, and various continental writers, as well as the 'philosophy of the moment' expounded by Walter Pater. But none of these rebellions against Victorianism achieved a redirection of poetry, however much they undermined the bases of moral complacency. Fundamentally they represented merely the other side of the coin of Victorian propriety, and there was no powerful re-examination of the realities of the cultural and human situation, and no new poetic vision.

There were, however, some Victorian poets who were to prove fruitful growing-points as far as the future was concerned. These were mostly poets inferior in actual technical resources or output to the great figures such as Tennyson and Browning, but who under the pressure of overwhelming personal emotion and experience forced a way through the preoccupations and verbal conventions of the age. There was, for example, the bleak cry of passion and suffering in a handful of the poems of Emily Brontë which sets her right outside the range of Victorian poetry as a whole—as in *Remembrance*:

> 'Cold in the earth—and the deep snow piled above thee,
> Far, far removed, cold in the dreary grave!
> Have I forgot, my only Love, to love thee
> Sever'd at last by Time's all-severing wave? . . .'

There is a similar unmistakable pressure of feeling, expressed in a more muted key but attended often by a disturbing and moving irony, behind such poems of Christina Rossetti as *Uphill*, *When I am dead my dearest*, and *Too late for love, too late for joy*. Christina Rossetti was a Pre-Raphaelite in so far as she wrote some of her poems under Keatsian and Italian influences, but the simplicity of language and imagery of some of her religious poems (influenced by the seventeenth-century poets Herbert and Vaughan), of some of her child poems, and of parts of her fairy-story *Goblin Market* is in refreshing contrast to the general run of Victorian verse.

There is no doubting the reality of feeling either behind Oscar Wilde's *The Ballad of Reading Gaol*, which in spite of its melodramatic passages has more authentic life in it than the work of the technically more accomplished Lionel Johnson, Ernest Dowson, and other poets of the 'decadence'.

It was T. S. Eliot who in 1941 rescued Rudyard Kipling from the neglect into which he had fallen, and largely as the result of his efforts it was realized that some of Kipling's poetry, particularly

Departmental Ditties and *Barrack Room Ballads*, had done something towards bringing English poetry back to 'the language really used by men'. In spite of the mechanical nature of his rhythms and his crudely journalistic effects Kipling's diction was certainly more lively than that of his contemporaries. His imperialism, moreover, was by no means the triumphant assertion of Victorian confidence it was once thought: on the contrary, it was shot through with the doubts and tensions of the *fin de siècle* and it had idealistic aspects in defence of which (as in the famous *Recessional*) Kipling set himself against some of the more menacing materialistic tendencies of the period. But at the human level he remained as immature as Swinburne.

There were, however, three poets in particular who pointed the way to the technical and imaginative renovation of which English poetry was in such urgent need. It was in 1898 that Thomas Hardy published his *Wessex Poems*. These owed something to the two volumes of poems in the Dorset dialect published in 1844 and 1859 by William Barnes, which contained a number of moving ballad-type lyrics. In Hardy's case the term 'lyric' is almost a misnomer, for his verses seldom 'soar' or 'sing'. Often they are prosaic, almost as if they were transcripts from the novels, and clumsy, sometimes downright ugly words, phrases, and rhymes are to be encountered in them. But the angularity is the expression of unmistakable force and integrity of character. These qualities come out in particular when he is re-creating intense personal experience in a vividly remembered context, whether this is a town, a street, a room, or the open countryside. In these re-creations there is no attempt to escape either into nostalgia or into a stoic posture: the past emotion, together with the emotion aroused by its contemplation, are examined and felt simultaneously, and in the process a genuine tragic sense emerges. One of the most remarkable features about Hardy's personality is its consistent, thorough-grained texture: the later poems have less bitterness than the youthful ones, but in both the control is firm and realistic. It is not surprising that the qualities of a poem like *Neutral Tones*, for example (written when he was in his twenties), should have exercised a considerable influence upon twentieth-century poets who were struggling to clear poetry of false emotion and inflated rhetoric:

> 'We stood by the pond that winter day,
> And the sun was white, as though chidden of God,
> And a few leaves lay on the starving sod,
> —They had fallen from an ash, and were gray. . .'

English Literature

The Victorian poet who made the greatest impact upon the poets of the 1920s, however, was Gerard Manley Hopkins. This was partly because his poems were not published until 1918, when the highly original technical devices and poetic approach expressed in Hopkins's 'short-hand' terms of 'sprung rhythm', 'instress', and 'inscape', coincided with other efforts to reform English verse. One of Hopkins's greatest services was to reintroduce the flexibility and variety of spoken language. In one of his letters (which in their acute recording of a poet's problems recall those of Keats) he told a friend not to read his poetry 'with the eyes . . . only', but to 'take breath and read it with the ears, as I always wish to be read, and my verse becomes allright'.

His use of language in fact was fundamentally dramatic in the way that Shakespeare's was, appealing not only to the eye and ear, but to the nervous and muscular sensations of the whole body. A characteristic example of this 'kinaesthetic' use of language is to be found in *The Leaden Echo and the Golden Echo*, which begins:

'How to kéep—is there any ány, is there none such,
      nowhere known some, bow or brooch or braid
      or brace, láce, latch or catch or key to keep
  Back beauty, keep it, beauty, beauty, beauty, . . .
      from vanishing away?'

Hopkins's own comment was: '*Back* is not pretty, but it gives that feeling of physical constraint which I want.'

As for Hopkins's religious poetry it reveals at its best an intensity of personal feeling, a clash of faith and despair, in complete contrast to the pulpit-manner of most Victorian religious poetry. It is in marked contrast, too, to the religiose verbosity (admittedly relieved by flashes of brilliance) of *The Hound of Heaven* by Hopkins's co-religionist Francis Thompson. Whereas Thompson's poem displays the influence of the seventeenth-century Crashaw blurred and debased, some of Hopkins's religious poems can without incongruity be set side by side with the *Holy Sonnets* of John Donne.

If, however, Hopkins was the Victorian poet who had the most influence upon the moderns, the natural link between the two eras was William Butler Yeats. His earlier work exhibited most of the characteristics of the poetry of the *fin de siècle*, and most of its influences, including those of Pater, the Aesthetic Movement, and the French Symbolists—and he was also intimately associated with

136

the Celtic Revival. The romantic pensiveness, the limpid water-
colour atmosphere of his early poems were very much to contemporary taste—though superior musical gifts as well as a strong
personal flavour were also evident in many of them. But Yeats
came to realize that he must discard most of the old influences,
and gradually he moved towards a barer, more supple use of
language better fitted to embody the realities of the times and of
his own experience:

> 'Through all the lying days of my youth
> I swayed my leaves and flowers in the sun;
> Now I may wither into the truth.'

The record of Victorian prose was far more creditable than that
of poetry. It was an age of very varied prose writing in many
departments, including those of history, religious and scientific
exposition, education, literary criticism, biography, autobiography, and travel—and there were many prose writers who, if
they had no practical solution to offer to the challenge of the times,
at least met it head on.

The ugliest form that this challenge assumed was that of the
philosophy of Utilitarianism, which, in a Hobbesian view of
human nature and society, involved the theories that well-being
could be scientifically arrived at by means of a 'felicific calculus',
that pestilence and famine were the natural regulators of over-
population, and that as immutable economic laws had established
the present division of the national income any interference—such
as humane poor laws or factory regulations—would upset the
economic balance.

The number of Victorians who accepted these findings in their
pure form was of course small. Indeed Utilitarianism itself was full
of paradoxes. The Benthamite idea of a kind of slide-rule for
securing the well-being of the greatest number in fact led to
important reforms in Parliamentary and local government, in
legal procedure, in sanitation and education, and in other fields.
But it was the principle of *laissez-faire* which underlay these theories
that was particularly powerful during the first half of the nineteenth century, affecting even enlightened Whig historians like
Lord Macaulay.

And obviously such a doctrine was to the interests of the middle
classes, since it appeared to make the untrammelled pursuit of
profit on the part of factory-owners a natural law, and—on strict

137

scientific grounds—positively discouraged efforts to improve the workers' lot.

The human and moral implications of these ideas were grim in the extreme—and they might have been worse if powerful voices had not been raised against them. One might have expected the most vigorous of these to proceed from the Churches. There were, of course, individual clergymen who did their best by precept and practice to mitigate the harsher aspects of Utilitarianism, and there was a good deal of private philanthropy and benevolence. But behind much of the religious thinking of the period, particularly that affected by Calvinism and the Evangelical Revival, lay the assumption that salvation was a matter of purely personal endeavour and that personal prosperity or poverty were preordained.

Certainly there were currents of religious thought that opposed the prevailing trend. There was the Christian Socialism of F. D. Maurice, and there was the idealist tradition of Burke, Scott, and Coleridge (Coleridge's views on Church and State had a considerable influence) which stressed traditional pieties and which set against the Hobbesian self-seeking of Utilitarianism the concept of an organic society such as had—it was supposed—existed in the Middle Ages.

Closely associated with this tradition was the Oxford Movement, which also stressed historic continuities, seeking to recover the Anglican spirit of the seventeenth century and to reintroduce ritual and colour (and—one is tempted to add—love) into Victorian worship. The defection to Roman Catholicism of its greatest supporter, John Henry Newman (who was also one of the greatest prose writers of the period), dealt a powerful blow to the movement—and also underlined the fact that the Victorian era was in a state of almost continuous religious crisis. For one thing, much of the religious controversy of the period was of an utterly arid nature, particularly in the field of biblical exegesis—a state of affairs reflected in George Eliot's unforgettable portrait of Casaubon and his soul-destroying labours in her great novel *Middlemarch*. The manifold religious doubts and confusions were apparent too, both in the spread of atheism and agnosticism and in the search, which became more frantic as the century progressed, for substitute religions, such as Theosophy. It was in this climate, too, that Eastern religions, particularly Buddhism and Hinduism, came to exercise an increasing appeal—and in which the religious ideas of Tolstoy found a sympathetic hearing.

The reassertion of Christian faith by so world-renowned a genius as Tolstoy, backed by the arguments of a powerful intellect, seemed indeed to offer one of the most serious counter-weights that the age afforded to the 'great challenge' that lay behind all the religious anxiety of the age. This challenge, of course, was that of the new science of Evolution, expounded by the geologist Sir Charles Lyell and others, and given its most memorable form in 1859 in Charles Darwin's *On the Origin of Species by Means of Natural Selection, or the Preservation of Favoured Races in the Struggle for Life*. Tennyson recorded something of the shock produced by the theories of Evolution in his *In Memoriam*, and towards the end of the century Julia Wedgwood described Darwin's book as a kind of wall stretching across her life and dividing it into two quite distinct halves.

As far as Utilitarianism was concerned, however, the most powerful protests came not so much from the leaders of the Churches as from thinkers such as Thomas Carlyle—who thundered against all those who worshipped only material progress, declaring that the age was entirely given over to the amassing of money and the pursuit of pleasure, plastering over the misery and pauperism created in the process with a sanctimonious optimism. Carlyle's castigations were delivered in a vehement, semi-biblical prose, sometimes contorted and eccentric, often eloquent and corrugated by rugged humour, recalling sometimes the Elizabethan Nashe, and sometimes the eighteenth-century Swift.

John Ruskin—whose prose style, though tending to inflation, also revealed something of the richness of the Elizabethans— carried Carlyle's campaign into the realm of aesthetics, denouncing the ugliness of an industrialized society founded upon abject poverty and a soulless attitude towards labour relations. Utilitarianism, Ruskin argued, could never be sound politics because it left out the vital human element. 'Any system which does not recognize the principle of the Brotherhood of Man', he insisted, 'is not political economy, but commercial economy', and he demanded—'May not the manufacture of souls of a good quality ... be worthy our attention' as well as that of trade goods?

Whereas Ruskin found the healthy social principles he sought in an idealized Middle Ages, Matthew Arnold argued that it was the classical spirit that was needed in order to attain harmony and comeliness in morals and culture, and it was for this reason that he recommended a revival of interest in 'the indispensable eighteenth century'. At the same time he argued that English taste needed to make contact with continental standards, introducing French writers hitherto little known and writing the first important article on the great Russian novelist Tolstoy. In Arnold's hands indeed literary criticism took on a new emphasis—for Arnold as for so many of the great critics that followed him culture was a serious business, 'the minister of the sweetness and light' that alone could mitigate the brutalizing effect of the 'Philistines' and 'Barbarians'.

The Aesthetic Movement of the 1890s, though its impact was weakened by dilettante tendencies, also set itself against the prevailing materialism of the age; Oscar Wilde, for example, recognized the importance of trying to reintegrate art and society and the fact that education should be concerned with people rather than facts.

Among other counter-weights to the materialistic spirit of the age must be mentioned John Stuart Mill's realization, recorded in his posthumous *Autobiography*, that the Utilitarianism in which he had been reared was deficient because it failed to give due place to the intuitions, the imagination, and the simple human feelings.

Although, however, the prose writers were more vigorous in their reactions to the challenge of the times than the poets, in their case too there were evasions and half-truths. Thus Carlyle, though at one time he was a Radical, came to distrust democracy and, under the influence of German writers, to advocate a doctrine close to the worship of pure power. Ruskin virtually cancelled out a telling piece of social criticism in *Unto this Last* by concluding: 'Note, finally, that all effectual advancement towards this true felicity of the human race must be by individual, not public effort.' In other words—the prevailing *laissez-faire* attitude extended even to many of those who were the most ardent opponents of Utilitarianism.

It was the realization by the working-class leaders that these allies had their middle-class reservations, that was in part responsible for turning them to more extreme forms of Socialism, including Marxism. Some of these issues were interestingly reflected in 'novels of social purpose' such as Charles Kingsley's *Alton Locke* and in the witty and imaginative novels of Benjamin Disraeli, who shrewdly recognized that Utilitarianism was fundamentally a doctrine for the thrusting middle classes and was just as alien to the interests of the landed aristocracy as to those of the working classes.

A number of other writers also used the novel for the explora-

an writer, ... day ... my play ...
has finished this little lyric, you
gave me the idea of, a couple of years ago.

"Put off this mask of burning gold
with emerald eyes"
"O no, my dear, you make so bold
To find if hearts be wild and wise
And yet not cold"

" I would but find what's there to find
love or deceit"
" It was the mask engaged your mind
And after set your heart a beat
not what's behind"

" But lest you be my enemy
I must enquire"
" O no, my dear, let all that be
what matter so there is but fire
in you, in me.

Part of an unpublished letter from W. B. Yeats dated 17 August 1910

Charles Dickens reading his own work

tion of social and political ideas or to reveal social conditions, among them Charles Reade, and, more notably, Mrs Gaskell. Mrs Gaskell was one of Dickens's favourite contributors to his periodicals—and it is, of course, Charles Dickens who more than anyone else fought the fact and the spirit of Utilitarianism. This remains true even though the weaknesses that went with Dickens's abundance and energy were such as might seem to disqualify him for a more serious role. In spite of his Hogarthian reforming zeal he showed little practical grasp as to what was needed to improve the lot of the lower classes, and his workmen are usually sentimentalized puppets. Throughout his career, moreover, his work tended to be extremely uneven. In *Martin Chuzzlewit*, for example, which contains in Mr Pecksniff the greatest study of hypocrisy and selfishness in English literature, and in which, George Gissing rightly declared, 'every quality of Dickens is seen at its best', there are passages of the most banal sentimentality.

Nevertheless the preoccupation with social issues was absolutely central to Dickens's inspiration, and in his second novel, *The Adventures of Oliver Twist*, Dickens began his long series of battles against the brutalities of officialdom, the evils of private education, the law courts, Government departments, the debtors' prison, conditions of childbirth, and many other abuses. Dickens in these novels was not primarily concerned with a factual analysis of Utilitarianism, though his satire was often quite explicit. Dickens's anger was directed above all against the soullessness of the system, its proneness to treat human beings not as individuals but as economic ciphers. It was the spirit of Utilitarianism he loathed even more than the fact.

Dickens's work, moreover, deepened as he grew older, gaining in power and concentration, and the novels of the 1850s—*Bleak House*, *Hard Times*, and *Little Dorrit* in particular—represent the peak of his achievement both in artistic control and in the force of his criticism. Dickens's characters have been denigrated on the grounds that they are simply Gillray-like caricatures: but the best of them are universal types like Chaucer's pilgrims and Ben Jonson's 'humours'. It must not be forgotten either that Dickens achieved these results by means of a style which, in spite of its excess of animal spirits, was one of the richest and most resourceful of the period.

The novel was the dominant literary mode of the Victorian Age, and for a number of years it had the kind of universal popularity that the drama had enjoyed during the Elizabethan period, catering for a wide range of interests at many different levels. As with the Elizabethan drama, too, with its beginnings in loose, episodic Chronicle Plays, the trend of the Victorian novel (as in the career of Dickens himself) was from a fairly simple organization of narrative elements to a profounder more poetic synthesis.

Much of the vast Victorian fictional output developed from that of the Romantic and Augustan periods. The historical novel inaugurated by Scott, for example, had a long line of descendants, and a number of the novelists of the first rank, including Dickens, George Eliot, and, most noteworthy, William Makepeace Thackeray, made excursions into historical fiction. Thackeray's *Vanity Fair*, however, is something much more than a novel about a group of upper-class people at the time of the Napoleonic Wars. In its own way it faced up to the realities of nineteenth-century life as surely as some of Dickens's novels. For the underlying theme is the fundamental hypocrisy and brutality of a world dominated by money and materialistic values. This theme is concentrated upon the marriage relationship, and particularly upon the contrast between the marriage relationship as it affects Becky and Amelia. And the reason the reader's sympathy goes out to Becky is because, in spite of her defiance and amorality, she is also a victim forced by a heartless society into a degrading position. One is reminded, too, of the tragic situation of the heroine in *The Woman in White* by Wilkie Collins (the pioneer of the modern detective story). The dilemma of Collins's heroine, social historians have pointed out, could hardly have arisen after the passing of the Married Women's Property Act, which in one respect at least afforded women a modicum of justice. This indeed was also the situation—or potentially so—of some of the heroines of Jane Austen's novels, and notably of Jane Fairfax in *Emma*.

The mention of Jane Austen places Thackeray in his correct context, for—though he possessed nothing like Jane Austen's power of ironic concentration—he was primarily an anti-Romantic, whose main influences were Addison, Goldsmith, and above all Fielding.

The Brontë sisters, on the other hand, belong very much to the Romantic tradition—though it is also significant that Charlotte Brontë dedicated the second edition of *Jane Eyre* to Thackeray. For her heroine is, after all, also the victim of a heartless and sanctimonious society which does its best to degrade her. Whereas Charlotte, for all her passionate rhetoric and feeling, remains a secondary figure completely bound to a Victorian view of life, there is no doubt that Emily Brontë's *Wuthering Heights* is one of the most remarkable works of genius of the period. It transcends the limitations of the standards of moral 'right' and 'wrong' applied by so many Victorian novelists and presents a highly poetic vision of 'good' and 'evil' in spiritual terms that few of her contemporaries seemed capable of understanding. It is a vision, too, which though personal, is objectivized, as a comparison with many of her more subjective poems shows. The machinery of the plot can, of course, be related to a very definite social context—property ownership, marriage as part of the property system, and the relationship of rich and poor—but the poetic force of the book demands of the reader a total response similar to that demanded by poetic tragedy of the order of *King Lear*, and some critics have even found a resemblance between the structure of this novel and Shakespeare's 'tragic pattern'. To describe the novel in terms of 'social propaganda' would be to belittle the intensity of Emily Brontë's vision of the spiritual values underlying human behaviour.

It was, however, George Eliot who carried the Victorian novel to its most mature achievements and at the same time brought to a close this particular phase in its development. One of the reasons for this is that the kind of broad-based popularity enjoyed by Dickens was, after 1870, nothing like as practicable. The growth of literacy was creating a vast new public whose state of mind was one that raised serious cultural issues. 'A weary public', Rider Haggard declared towards the end of the century, 'calls continually for books, new books to make them forget, to refresh them, to occupy minds jaded with the toil and emptiness . . . and vexation of our competitive existence.' In a competitive existence, too, it was only too easy for commercial interests to exploit the appetite for reading among the new and partially educated public.

By the time George Eliot published *Middlemarch*, in other words, the division into various 'brows' was well under way, and a serious writer was becoming increasingly obliged to avoid certain methods and certain areas of experience which had already become cheapened. George Eliot with her erudition and her friendship with philosophers such as Herbert Spencer and George Henry Lewes was indeed well qualified to be a 'high-brow' writer. But this does not mean that her work lacks either warm human qualities or humour.

Her seriousness evinced itself above all in her preoccupation with moral themes, and the fact that she had lost her religious faith had the effect of intensifying this concern—in a way that was to be of considerable importance for the future of English fiction. For in insisting that the individual, by the exercise of his moral discrimination, was in effect solely responsible for his own fate, she abolished 'plot'—in the old sense that it was something external to the protagonists. The focus of interest in George Eliot's novels (from *Adam Bede* onwards) was the moral choice made by her characters: character itself, in other words, became plot. It is one of her great triumphs that she was able to subject the motives and conduct of her characters to the most searching examination without sacrificing their essential humanity and reality or their firm attachment in a concrete social context. This is pre-eminently so of Dorothea, Casaubon, and Lydgate in *Middlemarch*, which in its scope and simultaneous handling of numerous related themes and characters comes nearer to Tolstoy's *War and Peace* than any other novel in the English language.

'Psychological realism' was helped forward by the advent of the French realists. Although at first they were greeted by cries of horrified protest—particularly in the case of Zola and the naturalists—gradually they were accepted. The naturalistic influence had a considerable effect in mitigating Victorian prudery, in jerking the English novel out of its insularity, and forcing it to focus more sharply on the social and political issues of the day. There was a period indeed during the last decades of the century when it must have looked as if the English novel was about to swing in the direction of French realism. A number of novels closely followed the methods of Zola and the naturalists, among them George Moore's *A Mummer's Wife* and Somerset Maugham's first novel, *Liza of Lambeth*. In addition many other novelists, including George Gissing, were indirectly affected by the techniques and atmospheres of the naturalists. But this type of realism was in fact fundamentally alien to English tastes, and a reaction set in, supported by the aesthetic movement, the Celtic Movement, the influence of the French symbolists, and other new currents of thought. At the same time, the earlier faith in the infallibility of science was weakened. Developments in biology, for example, tended to stress individual variation rather than natural selection, thereby modifying the Determinism which had been one of the main theories behind the characterization of Zola and the naturalists, and this was attended by a revival of 'idealism' in philosophy, criticism, and literature generally. It was in these circumstances, too, that the great Russian novelists, whose realism as Edmund Gosse put it was 'attended by pity and hope', began to replace the French as the major foreign influence in fiction.

After George Eliot, therefore, developments in English fiction on the whole pointed forward to the emergence of a new 'modern' type of novel. This is generally true of novelists still rooted in the old English traditions as well as of those more European or cosmopolitan in outlook. Samuel Butler's *The Way of All Flesh*, for example, was not at all revolutionary in form or technique, but when it was published posthumously in 1903 its bitter Voltairean exposure of the monstrosities of Victorian religious and patriarchal tyranny and hypocrisy dealt a tremendous blow at the tottering edifice of Victorian stability and self-confidence, as well as leading to a whole line of novels dealing with the revolt of the young against a stifling family background—D. H. Lawrence's *Sons and Lovers*, Somerset Maugham's *Of Human Bondage*, and James Joyce's *Portrait of the Artist as a Young Man* among them.

At one level, too, nothing could be more 'English' than Hardy's novels and stories about his native Wessex. His main theme was the conflict between the vanishing countryside with its immemorial bonds and customs, and the encroachments of industrialism and its materialistic values.

Hardy, however, was also a follower of George Eliot and imbibed similar philosophical influences; it was indeed the Determinism derived from Herbert Spencer and others, combined with the pessimism of Schopenhauer and the disenchanted nature of his own vision that led Hardy to the bleak view of human destiny—at the mercy of what he ironically called 'the President of the Immortals'—which heightened his tragic effects, although it also led to the clumsy accidents and coincidences that disfigure many of his novels. But, in spite of his 'Englishness', Hardy was influenced by the French realists, particularly Flaubert, and also by the Russians. In addition his tendency to treat character in its generic aspect—Tess, for example, is both a living woman and a symbol of a whole class and way of life in process of liquidation —pointed the way to later 'modern' techniques.

The immediate advance at this stage, however, was in the direction of psychological exploration in depth. Several novelists of the last decades of the Victorian era played their parts in this process, including George Gissing—particularly in his studies of the rootless, dispossessed characters of modern urban society— Anthony Trollope, who refused to take himself seriously as an artist but displayed a good deal of psychological penetration, and George Meredith, whose psychological subtlety and 'impressionistic' approach, though attended as Henry James pointed out by 'a fog of eloquence', anticipated the work of such 'poetic' novelists as Virginia Woolf and Elizabeth Bowen.

But the climax in the development of the English novel up to the outbreak of the First World War was represented by Henry James himself. The fact that—like T. S. Eliot—he was an American who became a British citizen had an important bearing on his work. For some of James's best novels dealt with the theme of the American attracted by the older and more sophisticated culture of Europe and finding, through bitter and often tragic experience, that moral issues and values were involved more complex than he (or more often she) had realized. These novels bore witness to the expansion of America after the Civil War, but the American expatriates in them also symbolized the increasing sense of uprootedness in a world heading for the cataclysm of world war. It was not a long step from James's novels to *The Waste Land* of T. S. Eliot.

The other major theme in James's work was the corruption, or attempted corruption, of the innocent by those who appear to possess the true values of cultivated living—and sometimes the two themes are combined as in *The Portrait of a Lady* (1881), probably James's greatest novel.

An important aspect of James's work was that he carried the criticism of the age a stage further: for it was not only the materialistic values of contemporary society that he exposed, but also the false aestheticism which had sprung up to mask them. In *The Spoils of Poynton*, for example, beautiful objects are themselves tainted by the manner of their acquisition and possession, and in other stories it is the artist himself who is corrupted, in one way or another, by the temptations of materialistic success. In other words, James pointed to one of the basic elements in modern culture—the increasing difficulty of the artist to maintain his integrity and independence.

This was a problem of which James had first-hand experience, and it partly explains his earnest, and sometimes compulsive, concern with 'the art of fiction'. No novelist submitted himself to a more rigorous apprenticeship or discoursed more fluently or cogently about it. His aim throughout was to explore the 'interesting' moral situation (which meant the reactions of his character to it) by means of that 'solidity of specification' which seemed to him essential. For a time he was an ardent disciple of the French

Realists, but came to the conclusion that they lacked 'the spiritual sense'. His final conclusion was that the best models for the serious novelist were Turgeney and George Eliot because they both exemplified 'solidity of specification' and 'the moral element' working at 'the very source of their inspiration'.

Technically James's peculiar contribution to the art of fiction was the elaboration of the 'dramatic novel', in which the narrator was almost completely eliminated. This led to some astonishing *tours de force* in which even description of scene and analysis of character and situation are conveyed through the 'points of view' of the various characters. Some of these achievements, it is true, are marred by an excess of technique and by the convoluted style for which James became famous. Often, however, one has the feeling that these were forms of defence against the encroachments of the material world, devices to protect his own integrity.

The main preoccupation of Joseph Conrad, the Pole who became a skipper in the British Merchant Service and one of the masters of English prose, was also the preservation of the moral integrity of the individual. But whereas James was a painstaking and subtle psychologist Conrad was primarily concerned with certain basic human values. 'Those who read me', he wrote, 'know my conviction that the world, the temporal world, rests on a few very simple ideas so simple that they must be as old as the hills. It rests, notably . . . on the idea of Fidelity.'

It is the 'fidelity' of his characters—their self-respect or steadfastness to their moral idea of themselves—that Conrad puts to the test in most of his novels and stories, usually against the background of the sea or the tropics (especially the sea) because here, it seemed to him, men were isolated from society and forced to face themselves and their own inner resources. Conrad's view of the human predicament was almost as bleak as Hardy's and often one feels that the concept of 'fidelity' is a frail enough protection against the forces that threaten it. In *Heart of Darkness*, indeed, it is thrust aside to reveal one of the most powerful evocations of evil and spiritual sterility in literature.

Conrad's vision of the corrupting power of what he called 'material interests' was as profound as that of James's. It is seen at its most impressive in *Nostromo* (1904) where the apparent advantages of material 'progress', in fact bring only spiritual emptiness and a gradual deterioration of moral discrimination and 'fidelity'.

The novels of James and Conrad clearly contain many of the qualities of great poetic drama. Both of them indeed wrote plays, but with only moderate success. Nevertheless by the time they were writing, the theatre was in a healthier condition than it had been for many years.

During the first part of the Victorian era several of the leading poets, including Tennyson, Browning, and Swinburne, tried their hands at writing for the theatre, but what they produced were academic exercises only. The common dramatic fare of the period was melodrama, presented with an excess of visual realism and in a highly rhetorical style of acting. The first symptom of a turn for the better was the production, in a new 'naturalistic' style, of T. W. Robertson's *Caste* in 1867, which in spite of wooden characterization and stilted dialogue at least dealt with topical issues. This phase was continued by the 'problem plays' of Henry Arthur Jones and Arthur Wing Pinero, which in fact made no real attempt to solve the largely artificial questions they posed, but—especially in the case of Pinero's 'well-made' plays—taught some badly needed lessons of dramatic structure and composition. None of these plays, however, compare in inherent vitality to those of Oscar Wilde, particularly *The Importance of Being Earnest*, which recaptured something of the wit and verve of Sheridan.

Wilde's greater vitality (like that of George Bernard Shaw) owed a good deal to the 'anti-Victorianism' of Samuel Butler— and to the reinvigorating influence of Henrik Ibsen, who was introduced to English audiences by a production of *The Doll's House* in 1889. The impact of the ideas contained in this and other plays was tremendous, and Ibsen has to be placed alongside such intellectual giants as Nietzsche, Schopenhauer, Tolstoy, Bergson, and Freud as one of the major foreign influences in the crumbling away of the old Victorian order and in the emergence of 'modern' culture.

Ibsen's greatest English disciple was Shaw, particularly as far as the treatment of topical issues was concerned. In technique Shaw set himself against the 'Irvingesque' approach, demanding a more serious type of play and a more naturalistic type of acting and production. His main concern, from his first play *Widowers' Houses* onwards, was, in the spirit of Molière, 'to chasten morals with ridicule'. His onslaughts on many of the cherished shibboleths of the day, including established religion, property, and capitalism, the 'purity' of women, and the sanctity of the married state, were reminiscent, in their blighting irony, of Tolstoy. Shaw's plays undoubtedly played an important part in dispelling some of the worst hypocrisies and evasions of the day, as well as restoring to

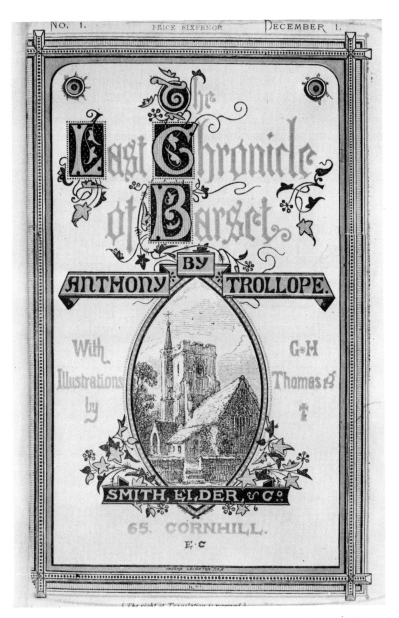

NO. 1.   PRICE SIXPENCE   DECEMBER 1.

The Last Chronicle of Barset

BY

ANTHONY TROLLOPE.

With Illustrations by

G.H Thomas

SMITH, ELDER & Co.

65. CORNHILL.

E. C

Illustrated wrapper for Trollope's *The Last Chronicle of Barset*, 1867

Ahenobarbus at Rehearsal, a drawing of G. B. Shaw in 1894 by Bernard
Partridge

English drama some of the vital social purpose it had possessed in the hands of such seventeenth-century dramatists as Ben Jonson. Although Shaw fails to convince when (as in *St Joan*) he attempts more emotional themes, he is in the great tradition of English comedy.

Other practitioners of the 'drama of ideas' were Granville-Barker and John Galsworthy, and playwrights such as Somerset Maugham, J. B. Priestley, James Bridie, James Barrie, and Noel Coward can all be seen as belonging, with varying degrees of skill and seriousness, to this tradition.

There were some, however, who believed that the revival of drama did not lie in this direction at all. Thus W. B. Yeats wrote of naturalistic drama: 'Except when it is superficial, or deliberately argumentative, it fills one's soul with a sense of commonness as with dust. It has one mortal ailment. It cannot become impassioned, that is to say vital, without making somebody gushing and sentimental.' John Millington Synge and Sean O'Casey also rejected the 'joyless and pallid work of the naturalistic drama'. Their aspirations were symbolized by Yeats's pronouncement that as the theatre 'began in ritual' it could not 'come to its greatness again without recalling words to their ancient sovereignty'—in effect without a revival of 'poetic drama'. This did not necessarily mean plays in verse—though in Yeats's case it did—but most of the plays produced at the Abbey Theatre in Dublin were informed with the spirit of poetry. Synge, for example, created out of the speech of the peasants of the Aran Islands a dramatic language as living as anything since the seventeenth century. *The Playboy of the Western World* (1907) is one of the great European plays of the century, while the one-act play *Riders to the Sea* (1904) was the first authentic example of tragedy in English drama for many years. Sean O'Casey's plays too, with their background of the Dublin slums and the Civil War, are full of an exuberance of language and action which by comparison reduces most of the 'naturalist' plays (apart from those of Shaw) to the dimensions of drawing-room drama.

In England poetic drama achieved no considerable results until the 1930s, when W. H. Auden and Christopher Isherwood collaborated in an attempt to blend elements of the popular theatre and serious comment on the contemporary political situation. It was in 1935, too, that T. S. Eliot wrote what is still the best of his verse plays, *Murder in the Cathedral*.

A successful poetic drama, of course, was impossible without a more supple and vital poetic language. The old habits were not easily abandoned and most Edwardian and Georgian poetry was derivative from the Victorians in style and approach. Most of the contributors to *Georgian Poetry*, a series of anthologies published between 1912 and 1920, deserved the nickname of 'week-end poets'. There were, however, some important exceptions. Walter de la Mare, for example, made effective use of the old traditions of the ballad, the popular song, and particularly of the nursery rhyme. In spite of his preoccupation with dream-like atmospheres, de la Mare's music was personal and authentic. Most of his nature poems, moreover, are the results of personal reflection and not a mere collection of echoes from Tennyson and Arnold, and the best of his child poetry re-creates something of the atmosphere—and tension—of Blake's *Songs of Innocence* and *Songs of Experience*. Some of W. H. Davies's nature lyrics, too, possessed a refreshing simplicity, while Edmund Blunden, having a more vital contact with the English countryside than most of his contemporaries, entered into the older tradition of realistic rural description represented by such poets as Cowper and Crabbe.

A similar quiet, unobtrusive realism marked the rural poetry of Edward Thomas. He is the poet not of romantic landscapes but of the village, the barn, the meadow, and the corner of the farmyard—and in *Adlestrop* he brings the urban world and the countryside into moving but unsentimental juxtaposition. The first stanza also raises another important consideration:

> 'Yes, I remember Adlestrop—
> The name, because one afternoon
> Of heat the express-train drew up there
> Unwontedly. It was late June.'

The language here is intimate, personal, unemphatic, colloquial, and yet at the same time full of lyrical feeling. It is a poetic diction similar in many respects to that of Hardy and of Robert Graves. D. H. Lawrence, in poems such as *End of Another Home Holiday*, might also be included in the same grouping—and it is one which points to the fact that there were forces within the native tradition itself making for a revitalization of English poetry.

A further impetus towards this revitalization was provided by the First World War. The earlier war poets, such as Julian Grenfell and Rupert Brooke, were on the whole typical Georgian poets (though their patriotism was utterly sincere and had not yet been smirched by cheap journalism), but the mounting holocaust

soon shocked poets out of the literary graces of suburban poeticiz-
ing. There was a purging anger in Siegfried Sassoon's:

> '. . . I'd like to see a Tank come down the stalls,
> Lurching to rag-time tunes, or "Home, Sweet Home"—
> And there'd be no more jokes in Music-Halls
> To mock the riddled corpses round Bapaume.'

What the shock of war had done to poetry was summed up by
the fragment of a Preface to the projected volume of poems which
Wilfrid Owen left unpublished at his death:

> 'Above all I am not concerned with Poetry.
> My subject is War, and the pity of War.
> The Poetry is in the pity.'

Here Owen was repudiating the romantic concept of 'Poesy' as
Keats (whom Owen resembles in many ways) had also done. His
poetry did not primarily reside in 'beauties' of rhythm or imagery,
separated from the pressure of a subject: the poetry *was* the pity.
Its immediacy lies in the tense, laconic diction, attended by a kind
of 'wit' or paradox that, as in *Greater Love*, recalls Donne or Marvell:

> 'Red lips are not so red
> As the stained stones kissed by the English dead. . .'

Futility, on the other hand, with its tragic irony and vivid sense of
life-in-death is reminiscent rather of Keats—or of the Elizabethan
Sir Walter Raleigh in the poems he wrote while awaiting
execution. Owen represents the peak of the 'trench poets' achievement, and only Isaac Rosenberg stands near him in power of
vision and originality of language and diction.

The later poetry of W. B. Yeats also contributed substantially to
the renovation of the native English tradition. He was, it is true,
absorbed in quite un-English preoccupations—in Gaelic mythology
and, towards the end of his life, in various esoteric philosophies and
in occultism—but what was particularly valuable as far as English
poetry was concerned was the directness and terseness of his verse,
particularly in the volumes published after 1918, and the irruption of
fierce individual feeling, as for example in *A Dialogue of Self and Soul*:

> 'What matter if the ditches are impure?
> What matter if I live it all once more?
> I am content to live it all again
> And yet again, if it be life to pitch
> Into the frogspawn of a blind man's ditch.'

English Literature

It was through poetry such as this that Yeats has exercised an influence upon modern English poetry that has equalled, if not surpassed, that of T. S. Eliot.

Nevertheless English poetry was also in need of the quite different revolution represented by T. S. Eliot and Ezra Pound. For one thing in the frantic, disjointed world of the 1920s the countryside could no longer provide sufficient dynamic or content. The modern city had to become the centre of poetic attention. This was part of the significance of T. S. Eliot's 1917 volume, which was entitled *Prufrock and Other Observations*. In these poems the sordid ugliness of modern urban life was, for the first time, presented with a realism that allowed no loophole for sentimental evasion. The rhythms of colloquial speech, often flattened out to produce a somnambulistic effect; the imagery drawn from the least 'poetic' aspects of contemporary life; the abrupt stops and starts, and the juxtaposition of grim ironic realism and flashes of lyrical beauty —these and other techniques derived in large part from French poets such as Baudelaire, Rimbaud, Laforgue, and Corbière. At the same time his poetry, especially in the passages of dramatic monologue, has affinities with the Metaphysical poets and with seventeenth-century drama.

The adoption of these techniques carried obvious implications. It meant a complete repudiation of the Tennysonian poetic stance, and of all attempts to dilute poetry to suit middle-class tastes. The poetry written by Eliot and Pound demanded alert intelligence and an ability to respond to a wide range of cultural references. On the face of it this suggests a link with the Aestheticism of the 1890s and the doctrine of 'art for art's sake'—and Pound's earlier poetry shows signs of these influences as well as of that of the Imagist Movement. But in *Hugh Selwyn Mauberley* (1920)—probably his greatest poem—he was in ironic control of his 'aestheticism' and was, like Eliot, directly commenting upon the realities of the contemporary cultural situation.

What Eliot and Pound were primarily concerned with was the demonstration of the breakdown of values and traditions in the post-war world. It is this feeling that lies behind their polyglot, cosmopolitan interests, such as that of Pound in the Far East and that of Eliot in Sanskrit and Hindi studies. But whereas Pound in his *Cantos* did not proceed much beyond this depiction of the fragmentation of cultures (pursued, however, with great erudition and in some memorable verse) and found his personal centre in Fascism, Eliot's response to the challenge of the times took a more profound course. Part of the greatness of *The Waste Land*, for example (which marks the climax of Eliot's earlier poetry), is that while it diagnosed the disintegration of Western civilization, and evoked a tremendously powerful vision of a breakdown not only of cultural values but of life itself, it did not yield to this vision. The waste land which Eliot depicted, in which 'nothing connects with nothing' also contained the implication that man must grope for contact with some vital principle that would renew the springs of human goodness and purpose. The poem, in fact, was already reaching out towards the next stage in Eliot's development, which was symbolized by *Ash Wednesday* (1930), the first considerable poem to be written after his religious conversion. This is by no means a poem of easy hope: the realities of the waste land are still present, and it rejects all short-cuts, but out of a sense of agonizing struggle emerges the promise of redemption:

> 'But the fountain sprang up and the bird sang down
> Redeem the time, redeem the dream
> The token of the word unheard, unspoken. . .'

From 1930 until the outbreak of the Second World War English poetry followed several lines of development. On the one hand there were the followers of Eliot and Pound, such as William Empson and Ronald Bottrall; on the other, the 'political' poets of the thirties—W. H. Auden, Cecil Day Lewis, and Stephen Spender —who were influenced more by D. H. Lawrence, Yeats, and— notably in the case of Day Lewis's quiet, tender lyrics—by Thomas Hardy. The poets of the latter group were united by their revolutionary beliefs, their use of Marxist and Freudian terminology, their sometimes effective use of contemporary slang and 'jazz' metres and rhythms and—in spite of a certain public-school cliqueishness—a genuine concern for the 'human situation'. The revolutionary aspect of their work reached its climax during the Spanish Civil War, though Spender's poems displayed an increasingly Shelleyan Romanticism and Auden's work became more freely interspersed with moments of lyricism. Louis Mac-Neice, though he did not respond to the appeal of Communism, was closely associated with this group, specializing in satirical commentaries upon the urban scene.

In 1936, however, a 'New Romanticism', as it has been called, made its appearance. It owed something to Edith Sitwell (whose own most significant poetic flowering did not take place until the early years of the Second World War) and also to Surrealism and the ideas of Herbert Read. Its most considerable exponents were George Barker, David Gascoyne, and Dylan Thomas.

Three of Thomas's small volumes were published between 1934 and 1939, and they were undoubtedly one of the most exciting literary phenomena since the 1920s. Thomas's torrent of words and images recall the phrase which Eliot applied to Tourneur: 'words perpetually juxtaposed in new and sudden combinations...' But this aspect of his work, in spite of its hypnotic appeal, is the least satisfactory. He was only superficially a 'Metaphysical' poet and his affinities were not so much with Eliot or Donne as with Hopkins and Blake. His real strength, which showed itself only intermittently, was in child-like, mystical evocations of the joy of living and of man's unity with his environment, particularly when these were concerned with his native Wales.

Finally, the years immediately before the outbreak of the Second World War witnessed the strengthening of the native English tradition, as that of Eliot and Pound tended to recede, under the influence of poets such as Edwin Muir and—most notably—Robert Graves. That the native tradition had come into its own was further demonstrated when Eliot began writing *The Four Quartets* which, in their meditative tone and in the evocative beauty of their lyrics, establish historic continuity with the past of English poetry as well as with the world of the 1920s.

As far as the novel was concerned, though James and Conrad had pointed the way to 'modern fiction', the tradition of the old solid Victorian novel still persisted at the same time that it struggled to embody foreign influences and the new pressures of a rapidly changing world. This is particularly noticeable in the cases of H. G. Wells, John Galsworthy, and Arnold Bennett. Wells, it is true, is rather a special case: he possessed far more creative vitality than the other two, and a vein of genuine poetic fantasy—which found an outlet in his scientific romances. His comedies of social life, particularly *Kipps* and *The History of Mr Polly*, were rooted in the tradition of Fielding, Smollett, and Dickens, and at the same time their theme of 'the little man' in revolt against a society which gives him inadequate educational and spiritual sustenance was (and is) thoroughly 'topical'. *Tono-Bungay*, one of his best novels, possesses tremendous energy and intelligence, and in its satire of the modern business world it has certain affinities with Conrad's *Nostromo*. But Wells regarded

154

himself as first and foremost an educator and prophet and he deliberately subordinated his other gifts. From about 1910 onwards he devoted himself almost entirely to propagandist novels, and though some of these contained vivid evocations of the intellectual and cultural ferment of the day, their general tendency was summed up, with characteristic asperity, by D. H. Lawrence: '. . . it is words, words, words, about Socialism and Karl Marx, bankers and cave-men, money and the superman. . . This book is all chewed-up newspaper, and chewed up scientific reports like a mouse's nest.'

Galsworthy certainly took himself seriously as a novelist. He studied foreign writers and in his desire to combine social realism with poetic feeling he was particularly susceptible to the influence of Turgenev—though during the period of 'the Russian fever', which raged from about 1912 to the end of the First World War, he also borrowed touches from Tolstoy and Dostoevsky, usually with ludicrous results. He can also be seen as to some extent a follower of James in his exposure, particularly in *A Man of Property*, of the withering effect of an obsessive concern for goods and bank balances upon the capacity for human relationships. But Galsworthy's novels marked no new departure technically, and as *The Forsyte Saga* progressed it became increasingly clear that Galsworthy was primarily a 'middle-brow' entertainer who shirked the radical issues.

The most painstaking of the English Realists of the period was Arnold Bennett, and although he too hankered after Russian sensibility, his main influences were the French Naturalists. The 'Clayhanger' series are important 'documentary' studies of life in the Potteries in the early years of the twentieth century, and *The Old Wives' Tale*, with its grasp of detail and locality and its sense of the slow lapses of time is one of the great novels of the century. Nevertheless it was Bennett above all who demonstrated that the limit of the old tradition in the English novel had, for the time being at any rate, been reached and that a new approach was needed that would implement the lessons implicit in the work of James and Conrad.

It was for this reason that Virginia Woolf seized upon Arnold Bennett as the prototype of the kind of novelist who was primarily concerned 'not with the spirit, but with the body', who spent 'immense skill and immense industry making the trivial and the transitory appear the true and the enduring'. In her view life was not 'a series of gig-lamps symmetrically arranged', but 'a luminous halo, a semi-transparent envelope surrounding us from the beginning of consciousness to the end'.

It was an approach that caught up many of the cultural currents of the period of the First World War and its aftermath, as well as expressing the sense of instability and flux as old values and conventions crumbled. It incorporated the influences of the Russians particularly of Dostoevsky, whose dramatically fluid techniques contributed considerably to the break-up of the old type of novel, and of Chekhov, who revolutionized the contours of the short story and influenced a whole host of post-war story writers, including Katherine Mansfield. Important, too, were the influences of Bergson's philosophy, of Freud and the theory of the subconscious, and of the Impressionist and Post-Impressionist painters.

All these influences tended to stress the individual human consciousness (with the subconscious below it) as the main arena of 'action', in opposition to the naturalistic point of view as represented by writers such as Bennett in which the individual is in the main shaped by his environment. They found their extreme form in the 'stream of consciousness' novels of Dorothy Richardson, in which there is no 'plot' in the accepted sense, but only a central consciousness reacting to the continuous flow of stimuli. Virginia Woolf's method was not dissimilar but involved much more subtlety and vitality and a far richer prose texture. The climax of this particular development was James Joyce's *Ulysses* (1922), especially in the final chapter where punctuation and third-person statement are abandoned and there are only the thoughts that drift into Molly Bloom's consciousness, until consciousness itself drifts into sleep.

Ulysses, of course, is far more than a 'stream of consciousness' novel. It is an incredibly detailed re-creation of a single day in the life of the city of Dublin and of a cross-section of its inhabitants, whose thoughts and destinies are linked in a complex network, causal, psychological, and verbal. It is also a great comic epic which at one and the same time symbolized the disintegration of twentieth-century culture and the eternal human predicament. *Finnegan's Wake*, however, on which Joyce worked between 1922 and 1939 suggested that this form of fiction too had come to a dead-end.

Another way of looking at Virginia Woolf's work is to see her as a representative of the liberal intellectuals of the period 'in between the wars' and the descendant of Victorians such as Ruskin, Arnold, and Mill, who spoke out against the brutalities of the society to

An informal picture of a 'Bloomsbury Group'. Left to right: Angelica Bell (Mrs Garnett), Vanessa Bell, Clive Bell, Virginia Woolf, Maynard Keynes

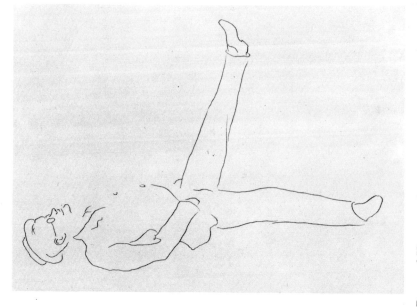

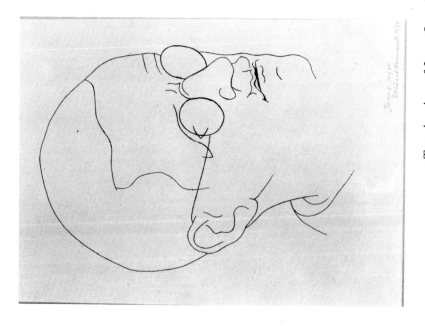

Two drawings of James Joyce by Desmond Harmsworth, 1932

which they belonged while still remaining an integral part of it. In Virginia Woolf's work, as in that of most of the Bloomsbury Group, there was, for example, a pervasive element that must be crudely described as 'snobbery'; it consisted mainly in the assumption that civilized values and sensibility resided only in a small *élite* and one, moreover, still related to a leisured upper-middle-class Edwardian background. In her work, too, appears an element that from now on, at any rate up to the outbreak of the Second World War, was to mark most of the novels of the liberal intelligentsia—an awareness of gradually encroaching violence accompanied by the suspicion that the psychic resources at their disposal were inadequate.

This interaction of private and humane values and meaningless violence is a common theme, too, in the novels of E. M. Forster. There are various factors, however, which place Forster in a different category from the Bloomsbury Group as a whole, and make him, in spite of the fact that his last novel was published as long ago as 1924, one of the most important of 'contemporary' novelists. One of these factors is the honesty and candour which allowed him to state calmly and undramatically: 'I belong to the fag-end of Victorian liberalism', and to ask: 'How on earth can an outlook which has lost its basis be any longer admirable?' The same integrity, indeed, led him to explain why he had stopped writing fiction: '. . . I had been accustomed to write about the old-fashioned world with its homes and family life and its comparative peace. All that went, and though I can think about the new world I cannot put it into fiction.'

Over and above this, Forster's profound belief in the 'holiness of the heart's affections'—symbolized by his phrase 'Only connect' —has been among the most positive affirmations of the twentieth century.

The sense of a shrinking area of civilized values threatened by violence and evil increased in intensity, however, as the Depression, the hunger marches, the rise of Nazism and Fascism, the Spanish War, and the menacing shadow of another world war forced themselves upon the consciousness of writers. In Aldous Huxley's novels even the small island of culture that remained is shown as fundamentally sterile and corrupt. Other aspects of the prevailing cultural and moral corruption were exposed, often in scenes of brilliant satirical comedy, in the novels of Evelyn Waugh, while it was in the 1930s that Graham Greene began his series of evocations of the contemporary scene in various

157

parts of the world, with their tremendous narrative verve and their remarkable sense of topical atmosphere and actuality—though it must be remembered that both these novelists were concerned not only with man in his relation to society, but also in his relation to God.

Among the most profound and comprehensive visions of modern society in fiction have been those of Wyndham Lewis and D. H. Lawrence. Lewis's was formed in the explosion of anger that succeeded the First World War: it is a pessimistic and largely destructive vision conveyed in terms of fable rather than realistic fiction. But it is a unified and dynamic picture of twentieth-century man and his predicament as a member of a mass civilization, as victim and participant in the 'age of the machine'.

D. H. Lawrence faced this predicament with more faith in man's potentialities to 'win through' to psychic health. In many respects Lawrence was a thoroughly 'traditional' writer; most of his influences were English and he was hostile to the French Realists —though he undoubtedly owed something to Tolstoy and Dostoevsky. He was not, in fact, an 'experimental' writer in the usual sense of the term. The revolutionary nature of his fiction derived fundamentally from the force and originality of his genius. What he was above all concerned with was to reveal the true springs of man's vitality that would alone enable him to transform both his inner life and his environment. These he believed were not available to the intellect; they could be discovered only by direct intuition, by 'knowledge' gained at the instinctual level. The importance of sex to Lawrence was that it was one of the avenues (there were others, such as nature, the life of animals, and death itself) leading to this deeper knowledge. The body, in fact, according to Lawrence could reveal the truth about man's being as the intellect, divorced from the body, could never do.

In his novels and stories therefore (and often in his poems) Lawrence was exploring the essential differences between those who are in direct contact—even if only fitfully—with this source of vitality—as with Ursula and Birkin in *Women in Love*—and those who fail to find it or substitute for it the false 'strength' of the will or the intellect—as with Hermione, Gudrun and Gerald. It was in *The Rainbow* and its sequel *Women in Love* that Lawrence explored these themes in greatest depth, relating them not only to the destinies of the individual characters and of successive generations, but also to the whole of twentieth-century England as the older rural ways of life, and the moral and religious props that supported them, were submerged in the rising tide of urbanization.

Lawrence's technical originality grew directly out of these preoccupations. As he was concerned primarily with the degree to which his characters were in touch with 'the body's life' his interest in their actions was not that of the ordinary novelist. 'I have a different attitude to my characters', he wrote about *The Rainbow*, 'I don't care so much what the woman feels . . . that presumes an ego to feel with. I only care what the woman *is*. . . You mustn't look in my novel for the old stable ego of a character. There is another ego, according to whose action the individual is unrecognizable, and passes through, as it were, allotropic states . . .'

In consequence Lawrence had no use for what he called the 'skin and grief' form of the average contemporary novel. In his most characteristic work he was employing an entirely new kind of narration, with a far freer, looser kind of organization which captured the rhythms and respirations of this inner reality. More than any other modern writer Lawrence was aware of Man's predicament when he is cut off from the true sources of vitality. More than any other he strove to affirm and renew life. More than any other he tried to meet the danger pointed out by Carlyle nearly a hundred years before, that in the 'machine age' men might only too easily grow 'mechanical in head and heart, as well as in hand'. Both in form and content, therefore, Lawrence represented one of the most determined attempts to grapple with the basic problems of the times—and one of the most fruitful challenges for the future.

How that challenge has been met—or evaded—lies outside the scope of this inquiry, which has deliberately halted on the eve of the Second World War. Important work has of course been written since then, both in poetry and in prose, some of it in the traditions of the writers just discussed, some of it in those of our older writers, and some that has broken new ground. But it is still too close to us, still too much a matter of subjective response for it to be possible to approach it with the kind of detachment that one must at least try to achieve in a book that aims at a 'perspective' of English literature. The writers of the '20s and '30s, however, are already sufficiently distant for us to end on the positive affirmation that our century in retrospect is likely to prove as vital and varied a period as any in our literary history.

Acknowledgements

The publishers wish to thank the following for permission to reproduce the illustrations shown by facing page references: The Master and Fellows of Trinity College, Cambridge, *frontispiece*; The Huntington Library, San Marino, California, 17, 21; Devonshire Collection Chatsworth. By permission of the Trustees of the Chatsworth Settlement, 52; The Master and Fellows of Magdalene College, Cambridge, 69; Victoria & Albert Museum. Crown Copyright, 92; From 'Poets Corner' by Max Beerbohm, by kind permission of Messrs. William Heinemann Ltd and by courtesy of the Trustees of The Tate Gallery, London, 132; The Raymond Mander and Joe Mitchenson Theatre Collection, 149; Mr Leonard Woolf, 156; The Lord Harmsworth of Egham, 157; Mrs W. B. Yeats, 140; The Trustees of the British Museum, 11, 16, 29, 37, 44, 53, 68, 84, 100, 101, 117, 148; Radio Times Hulton Picture Library, 10, 45, 60, 61, 85, 93, 108, 109, 116, 125.